SAGE

Gillian Giles

COMPU STEP

The Community College of Kent

In easy steps is an imprint of Computer Step
Southfield Road . Southam
Warwickshire CV47 OFB . England

Tel: 01926 817999 Fax: 01926 817005
http://www.computerstep.com

Reprinted 1999

Notice of Liability

Trademarks

Printed and bound in the United Kingdom

ISBN 1-84078-017-7

Contents

1	**Getting Started**	**7**
Introduction	8
Starting Sage Line 50	9
Settings	10
Company Preferences	11
Currency & the Euro	14
Customer & Supplier Defaults	15
Finance Rates	17
The Sage Line 50 Toolbar	18

2	**The Customer Ledger**	**19**
The Importance of Keeping a Financial System	20
The Customers Toolbar	21
Creating Customer Records	22
Batch Customer Invoice	24
Batch Customer Credit Note	25
Debtors Analysis	26
Credit Charges	27
Disputed Invoices	28
Customer Reports and Phone	29
Customer Letters and Labels	30
The Customer Statement	32

3	**The Supplier Ledger**	**33**
The Supplier Toolbar	34
Creating Supplier Records	35
Using Criteria	36
Supplier Activity	37
Supplier Aged Balance	38
Recording Supplier Invoices	39
Recording Supplier Credit Notes	40
Supplier Letters and Labels	41
Supplier Reports	42

4	**The Nominal Ledger**	**43**
The Nominal Toolbar	44
The Nominal Ledger	45
Nominal Records	46

Viewing Nominal Transactions   47
The Journal   50
Making a Journal Entry   51
Setting up Prepayments   52
Setting up Accruals   53
The Chart of Accounts   54
Nominal Reports   56

5 The Bank   57

The Bank Toolbar   58
Bank Accounts   59
Bank, Cash and Credit Accounts   60
Recording Bank Payments   61
Supplier Invoice Payments   62
Batch Purchase Payments   63
Bank Receipts   64
Recording Customer Receipts   65
Bank Transfers   66
Recurring Entries   67
Generating Cheques   68
The Bank Statement   69
Bank Account Reconciliation   70
Bank Reports   72

6 Products   73

The Products Toolbar   74
The Product Record   75
Product Defaults   78
Using Criteria   79
Bill of Materials   80
Viewing Transactions   81
Product Activity   82
Product Adjustments   84
Product Transfers   85
Product Reports   86

7 Invoices   87

The Invoicing Toolbar   88
Invoicing   89
The Product Invoice   90
Printing an Invoice   92
The Service Invoice   93

The Skeleton Invoice   95
Product Credit Note   96
Service Credit Note   97
Updating your Ledgers   98
Printing for Batch Invoicing   99
Producing Reports   100

8   Processing Sales Orders   101

The Sales Order Processing Toolbar   102
The Sales Order   103
Allocating Stock   105
Despatching Sales Orders   106
Amending & Printing Sales Orders   107
Sales Orders Reports   108

9   Purchase Orders   109

Purchase Order Processing Toolbar   110
Creating a Purchase Order   111
Placing Purchase Orders 'on order'   113
Recording Deliveries   114
Processing Purchases Manually   115
Recording Deliveries Manually   116
Printing Batched Purchase Orders   117
Purchase Order Reports   118

10   Financials   119

The Financials Toolbar   120
The Audit Trail   121
The Trial Balance   123
Profit and Loss Report   124
The Balance Sheet   125
Quick Ratio Report   126
The Budget Report   127
The Prior Year Report   128
The VAT Return   129
Financial Reports   132

11   Fixed Assets   133

The Fixed Assets Toolbar   134
Recording your Fixed Assets   135
Fixed Asset Depreciation   137
Depreciation and Valuation   138

12	**The Report Designer**	**139**
	Introducing the Report Designer	140
	Creating a new Report	141
	Modifying an existing Report	144

13	**Opening Balances**	**145**
	Introduction	146
	Opening Balances – Standard VAT	147
	Opening Balances – VAT Cash Accounting	148
	Clearing Opening Balances from Trial Balance	149
	Entering Balances Part Way through the Year	151
	Nominal Ledger and Bank Account	152
	Opening Balances for Products	154

14	**Data Management**	**155**
	Backing up Data	156
	Restoring Data	157
	Changing Global Values	158
	Importing Data	160
	File Maintenance	162
	Write Off, Refund and Return	165
	Posting Contra Entries	168
	Run Period End Functions	169
	Clearing the Audit Trail and Stock	172

15	**The Task Manager**	**173**
	Features of the Tasks Option	174
	The Task Manager Desktop	175
	Setting up a To Do task	176
	Recording a new Bill	177
	Paying a Bill	178
	Accounts Due	179
	Account Status	180
	The Recurring Option	181
	Stock Option	182
	Invoices Option	183
	Sales Order Processing	184
	Purchase Order Processing	185
	The Company Stack	186

Index		**187**

Getting Started

This chapter takes you through the stages of preparing the new Sage Line 50 for use. It explains initial procedures for setting up defaults required by the program.

Covers

Introduction | 8

Starting Sage Line 50 | 9

Settings | 10

Company Preferences | 11

Currency & the Euro | 14

Customer & Supplier Defaults | 15

Finance Rates | 17

The Sage Line 50 Toolbar | 18

Chapter One

Introduction

This book covers Sage Line 50 Accountant, Accountant plus and Financial Controller.

All businesses need to keep accurate records of their accounts, but even with a computer program, if the information is not entered correctly, then the accounts could still be wrong. After all, it's easy to blame the computer!

Working through Sage Line 50 in easy steps

This book explains in simple, easy stages how to perform the main tasks required for keeping computerised business accounts. The following chapters show how to:

* Set defaults and Company preferences.

Accuracy reduces errors and prevents costly mistakes.

* Create customer & supplier records.

* Set up opening balances, maintain Bank accounts.

* Maintain the Nominal Ledger and run an audit trail.

* Generate sales orders and control stock.

* Print invoices, credit notes and statements.

* Produce history and financial reports.

'Preparing to start' checklist

Before getting started with Sage Line 50 work through the checklist below.

Some things, such as the start date for the financial year, once entered cannot be changed, so do make sure you have all relevant information to hand before using Sage Line 50 for the first time.

* Check the start date of your company's financial year.

* Check with an accountant which VAT scheme is used.

* Draw up a list of defaults to use.

* Decide on users and passwords.

* Backup the data if updating Sage.

* Have customer, supplier and bank details to hand.

* Product details, recommend a stock take.

* A list of all opening balances.

Starting Sage Line 50

Turn on your computer and wait for the Windows Desktop to appear. To start Sage Line 50 do the following:

1 Click on Start.

2 Point to Programs – a selection appears.

3 Point to Sage.

 Altern-atively, if a shortcut has been set up on the Windows desktop, you can open Sage Line 50 by double-clicking on the icon.

4 Click on Sage Line 50.

The Sage Line 50 desktop appears:

 If Sage Line 50 has been installed for the first time the installation wizard will place it in a folder called Line 50. If you are upgrading from Sage Sterling, Line 50 will be placed in the original SFW folder.

Settings

Before Sage Line 50 can be used there are a number of settings and defaults that need to be entered. The rest of this chapter shows how to do this. When required, select the appropriate settings option from the following list:

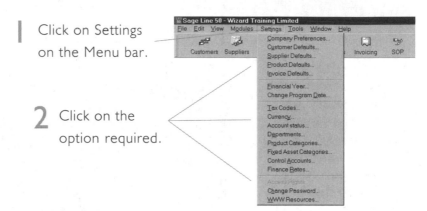

1 Click on Settings on the Menu bar.

2 Click on the option required.

Using Passwords

The Data Protection Act requires that any system containing confidential information, i.e., financial details etc., should be protected against unauthorised access. Sage Line 50 uses a password to achieve this. Once you set a password, Sage Line 50 always prompts you for it at startup.

As with any password, you should never write it down if it can be avoided. Therefore, try to choose a password that is both easy for you to remember but difficult for someone else to discover. You can decrease the chance of somebody accidentally finding out your password by using a mixture of letters and numbers instead of an actual word.

1 From the Settings menu click on Change Password.

2 Type your password here.

3 Repeat the password here for confirmation.

4 Click OK to save password.

Company Preferences

When you ran Sage Line 50 for the first time the Easy Startup Wizard asked for your Company details. Alternatively, after selecting Company Preferences from the settings options, you can enter these details as follows:

Use the Tab key instead of your mouse to move onto the next line or box.

1 Enter your company name here.

2 Enter your full address details in this box.

3 E-Mail and Web addresses go here.

4 Enter VAT & Credit Ref No's. if appropriate.

5 Remove if not required.

6 Click OK to finish.

Departments, Product and Fixed Asset Categories

For analysis purposes, you can assign transactions to different departments and divide products and fixed assets into different categories. To set up each of these:

You can assign your transactions to up to 999 different departments and divide Products into 999 different categories. Sage Line 50 also lets you divide Fixed Assets into 100 different categories for analysis & reporting purposes.

1 Click on the required settings option & select the first blank entry.

2 Click Edit to bring up the Edit box.

3 Enter appropriate name.

4 Click OK.

5 Repeat steps 1–4 for Products & Fixed Assets.

...cont'd

Setting up & checking Tax Codes

Sage Line 50 already has the standard UK and EC VAT Rates set for you together with the code T1 (standard rate – currently 17.5%) set as the default tax code. Here is a list of the codes automatically set up during installation:

T0 – zero rated transactions
T1 – standard rate
T2 – exempt transactions
T4 – sales to customers in EC*
T7 – zero rated purchases from suppliers in EC*
T8 – standard rated purchases from suppliers in EC*
T9 – transactions not involving VAT

(* Outside the UK)

It is important to use the correct VAT codes. If unsure of current UK or EU VAT Tax rates then contact Customs & Excise.

There are 99 VAT codes available in Sage Line 50. To enter or change VAT tax rates:

T1 is the standard rate code.

Code	Rate	In Use	EC Sale	EC Purch
T0	0.00	Y	N	N
T1	17.50	Y	N	N
T2	0.00	Y	N	N
T3	0.00	Y	N	N
T4	0.00	Y	Y	N
T5	0.00	Y	N	N
T6	0.00	Y	N	N

1 Choose Tax Codes after clicking on Settings on the menu bar, then select the required code.

2 Click Edit to bring up the Edit Tax Code box.

3 Enter percentage rate.

4 Click here if VAT rate is for an EC Code.

5 Select an EC Purchases & Sales link if appropriate.

6 Click OK, then Close the Tax Codes box.

12 Sage Line 50 in easy steps

...cont'd

Financial Year

The start of the financial year is entered during the installation of Sage Line 50 or before entering any transactions:

 Once transactions have been posted, the Financial Year cannot be changed.

1 From Settings on the menu bar click on Financial Year then select the first month of your year from the list.

2 Enter the year if not correct.

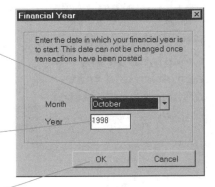

3 Click OK.

Account Status

A new feature within Sage Line 50 is that you can assign an account status to each of your accounts. You can add an account status at any time to the ten already set up:

 Account Status is a useful new feature recently added to Sage Line 50. Use this facility to mark accounts which are bad debts or have exceeded their credit limit, and for placing orders on hold if necessary.

1 Click on Account status from the Settings options then highlight the next available blank status line.

2 Click Edit.

3 Enter Status Name here.

4 Click here if you want this status to place accounts 'on hold'.

5 Click OK to save this new status, then Close.

Currency & the Euro

Initially Sage Line 50 is already set up with the currencies of the EC countries. These details can be edited or other countries set up as required:

Simply press F5 to access the Euro Calculator in any numeric field that displays a calculator button.

1 Click on Settings > Currency and highlight the currency you want to edit or select the first available blank record to enter a new currency.

No	Name	Country	EC	Ex. Rate	EMU	EMU Rate
1	Pound Sterling	United Kingdom	GB	0.000000	No	0.000000
2	Belgium Franc	Belgium	BE	0.000000	No	0.000000
3	Krona	Denmark	DK	0.000000	No	0.000000
4	French Franc	France	FR	0.000000	No	0.000000
5	German Mark	Germany	DE	0.000000	No	0.000000
6	Drachma	Greece	EL	0.000000	No	0.000000
7	Punt	Ireland	IE	0.000000	No	0.000000
8	Lira	Italy	IT	0.000000	No	0.000000

Sterling to Euro rate   0.000000   Edit   Close

2 Click Edit to bring up the Edit Currency box.

3 Enter the name of the Currency.

The calculator can be used to either view an amount converted from Sterling to a Euro/Foreign Currency or to convert a Euro/ Foreign Currency amount to Sterling.

4 Enter the Country here.

5 The EC Member code goes here.

6 Enter the Currency exchange rate.

Edit Currency

Currency Details

Currency   Pound Sterling

Country   United Kingdom

EC Member   GB

Rates

Ex. Rate   0.000000

☐ EMU Member

EMU Rate   0.000000

OK   Cancel

7 Select this box if country is a member of the EMU.

8 Enter the Euro conversion rate here.

9 Click OK, then Close the Currencies box.

Customer & Supplier Defaults

When creating a new customer or supplier, details about credit limit, terms, discount etc. are needed. Customer and Supplier records are fully discussed in Chapters Two & Three respectively but before this, however, defaults need setting up.

For customers, default nominal codes (N/C) start at 4000.

1 Select Customer Defaults from the Settings options.

2 Select this Tab to enter the defaults for your customer records.

3 Click on the relevant Tabs to enter Statements, Ageing Balance and Discount defaults.

4 Click OK to save Customer Defaults.

5 Select Supplier Defaults from the Settings options.

Default nominal codes for suppliers start at 5000.

6 Enter relevant Supplier Defaults here.

7 Select this Tab to enter Aged Balances Period, specifying calendar months or days.

8 Click OK to save Supplier Defaults.

Product Defaults

Defaults also need to be set up for Products:

| Select Product Defaults from the Settings options.

You can use the Finder button on the right of the Nominal Code box to speed up entry.

The Finder button is also a quick way of creating a new Nominal Code.

2 Enter the Nominal account code here.

3 Allocate the correct Tax Code for the Product.

4 Complete the rest of the defaults as necessary.

5 Enter the Decimal Point placing for the product.

6 Click OK to save this information.

Control Accounts

Sage Line 50 uses Control Accounts to make automatic double-entry postings to the ledger.

Unless you have created your own Chart of Accounts, the Control accounts should never need changing.

| To view or edit these Nominal Codes select Control Accounts from the Settings options.

2 To change a Control account click on the nominal code and type the new code or use the Finder button.

3 Click OK to save and close or Cancel to abandon changes.

Control Accounts

Control Account	N/C
Debtors Control	1100
Creditors Control	2100
Default Bank	1200
VAT on Sales	2200
VAT on Purchases	2201
Sales Discount	4009
Purchase Discount	5009
Retained Earnings	3200
Default Sales	4000
Accruals	2109
Prepayments	1103
Bad Debts	8100
Mispostings	9999

Finance Rates

Finance rates need to be set up before any credit charges can be applied to your customers.

When a Finance Charge Rate is applied to a transaction, the first rate charged will be applied monthly until the invoice is paid.

1 Click on the Finance Rates option from the Settings menu to bring up the Finance Charge Rates box.

2 Click on Add to enter a new finance rate charge.

3 Enter the date the charge is to be applied from.

4 Enter the Base Rate as a percentage here.

Use the Delete button on the Finance Charge Rates window to remove any unwanted charges.

5 Enter an additional charge here if applicable.

6 Click OK to save new finance rate or Cancel to return to the Finance Charge Rates box.

7 Click Close to finish.

The Sage Line 50 Toolbar

From the toolbar the user selects an accounting option by clicking on the relevant button. Alternatively, the required function can be selected from the Modules option on the Menu bar.

 If any of the Toolbar options do not appear onscreen, click on the arrow button on the left or right of the Toolbar to display them.

 To make the buttons more distinct, select Tools then Options from the menu bar, then check the Show Button Frames box.

 For quick access to the Sage Web site, just click on the Internet button.

 Opens the Customer (sales) Ledger.

 Opens the Supplier (purchase) Ledger.

 Opens the Nominal Ledger.

 To access the Bank, Credit Cards and Petty Cash accounts.

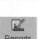 Opens the Product Records and Stock accounts.

 To generate Invoices, Credits and related reports.

 To generate Sales Order Purchases and reports.

 Opens the Purchase Order Processing window.

 To access Financial functions (i.e., Profit & Loss, Audit Trail, Trial Balance, VAT).

 To access Fixed Assets information and reports.

 Opens the Report Designer window.

Opens the Sage Line 50 Task Manager window.

Runs the Internet Browser.

Brings up a menu of Wizards options.

Brings up a menu of Help options.

The Customer Ledger

In this chapter you will learn how to use the Customer (Sales) Ledger to maintain customer records and create new ones as well as entering credit notes and invoices. You will also be shown how to view transaction activity as well as produce an overdue payments letter, and will learn how to apply credit charges and to mark an invoice as disputed.

Covers

The Importance of Keeping a Financial System | 20

The Customers Toolbar | 21

Creating Customer Records | 22

Batch Customer Invoice | 24

Batch Customer Credit Note | 25

Debtors Analysis | 26

Credit Charges | 27

Disputed Invoices | 28

Customer Reports and Phone | 29

Customer Letters and Labels | 30

The Customer Statement | 32

Chapter Two

The Importance of Keeping a Financial System

It is essential for all businesses to have a system to record and monitor their business and financial transactions. This information needs to be accurately recorded and kept up to date if it is to present a true financial position.

Such a system will involve the recording of transactions using the traditional method of bookkeeping or advanced accounting procedures, where financial reports (i.e., profit & loss statements and balance sheet, etc.) can be produced.

These reports provide Management with information on sales, purchases, turnover, expenses, debtors and creditors, assets and liabilities, and more importantly, if the business has made a profit.

The Inland Revenue and HM Customs & Excise (if VAT registered) will also need accurate accounts, which must conform to general bookkeeping and accounting procedures.

This information is also of importance to your Bank Manager, especially if there is a need to borrow money to ease cash flow problems or help set up a new business venture. Likewise, potential investors in your business may first want to see the true financial position of your accounts before making a decision.

Computerised systems have now removed the majority of time consuming and repetitive tasks of manual accounting. Businesses can check their financial status on a daily basis, or over a designated period of time. This valuable information will aid important decision making and business planning and is crucial for forecasting whether a business will succeed or fail.

The Customers Toolbar

The Customers toolbar provides features for creating customer records, viewing the activity of customer transactions, producing invoices and credit notes, marking invoices in dispute and applying credit charges. Customer Statements are produced here as well as letters and a wide range of reports.

 Creates a new Customer Account.

 Opens a Customer Record.

 Opens Customer Activity.

 Opens Customer Aged Balances.

 Opens the Batch Customer Invoices window.

 Opens the Batch Customer Credits window.

 Opens the Disputed Items window.

 Opens the Credit Charges window.

 To automatically Dial a Customer.

 To print Customer Labels.

 To print Standard Letters to Customers.

 To print Customer Statements.

To run Customer Reports.

Creating Customer Records

 Use the New wizard for simple step by step instructions for entering a new customer record.

Within this window, a customer record can be added, edited or deleted. You can also record agreed credit terms and even log any contact you have with a customer, such as telephone calls and who you spoke to.

1 Select Customers from the Sage Line 50 toolbar, then click on Record to bring up the Customer Record window.

 Always start by entering the Account Code first. Each customer is given a unique A/C code of up to 8 characters. Use the finder button to locate existing codes.

2 Use Details to store customer name, address and contact information.

3 Use the O/B button to enter an Opening Balance where required.

 Before you enter an Opening Balance you must have first saved the new customer details.

Sage Line 50 - Wizard Training Limited - [Customer - Palmer Energy Ltd]

File　Edit　View　Modules　Settings　Tools　Window　Help

| Customers | Suppliers | Nominal | Bank | Products | Invoicing | SOP | POP | Financials | Assets |

Details | Defaults | Credit Control | Sales | Graphs | Activity | Contacts | Memo

A/C	PEL01
Name	Palmer Energy Ltd	Telephone	01987 345345
Street1	Energy House	Telephone 2	
Street2	123 Edison Road	Fax	01987 345346
Town	Hightown	E-Mail	avolt@palmer-energy.com
County	Highshire	WWW	www.palmer-energy.com
Post Code	HI8 9GH		
Contact name	Alan Volt	Acc.Status	00 - Open
Trade contact			
VAT Number			
Balance	0.00 %		Delivery...

Save　Abandon　Delete　Back　Next　Close

 The method of entering opening balances is different for Standard VAT and VAT Cash Accounting. Use F1 help key to check.

4 Use the Credit Control tab to enter credit terms agreed with the customer.

5 Select Account Status from this drop down box.

6 Click Save to store the Customer Record.

7 Enter a new record or click Close to finish.

...cont'd

Use Activity to quickly view a customer's outstanding balance, Aged Debts etc.

These codes identify the transaction type:

SI = Sales Invoice

SR = Sales Receipt

SC = Sales Credit Note

SD = Discount

SA = Sales Receipt on Account

Use the Tidy button to clear all transaction sub-items from view.

To view this screen from the Customers window, select the customer required and then click on the Activity button.

Viewing transactions

Once customer activity has taken place, Sage Line 50 offers you a variety of options for checking customer transaction details:

- View customer invoices, receipts, credit notes and balances on a monthly basis, as a graph or table.

- Use the Activity option to see a breakdown of each customer's transactions.

- View or print the Customer's aged balances.

1 Click on the Activity tab in the Customer Record window.

No		Tp	Date	Refn	Details	Amount	O/S	Debit	Credit
1005		SC	27/10/1999	Cancel	Cancel - see tran 997	2291.25	2291.25 *		2291.25
1006		SI	10/07/1999	252	Maintenance	200.49	200.49 *	200.49	
1007		SI	15/11/1999	310	Training	916.50	916.50 *	916.50	
1010		SI	14/11/1999	313	Training	114.56	114.56 *	114.56	
		SC	15/11/1999	134					
1011				4001	Cancel - see tran 234	11.46	11.46 *		11.46

A/C: BUS001
Name: Business Exhibitions
Credit Limit: 4000.00
Balance: 720.59
Amount Paid: 11100.00
Turnover YTD: 1610.00

Future	Current	1 Month(s)	2 Month(s)	3 Month(s)	Older
0.00	1019.60	-2291.25	0.00	0.00	1992.24

2 Double click on a transaction to show all items.

3 Click on the arrows to scroll through all the transactions.

4 Click on Range to select another date range or range of transactions, then click OK.

5 Select Close to return to Customer window.

Batch Customer Invoice

Invoices are important business transaction documents and record detailed information about the goods or services supplied to the customer. Briefly, these details include the invoice number, name and address of the customer, date of sale, details of goods and or services supplied, details of discount, total amount of money due and terms of trade.

There are different types of invoices for the task you are carrying out and Chapter Seven shows you how to create a product or a service invoice, as well as automatically creating an invoice from a sales order. However, any invoices produced manually (Batch Invoices) and sent to customers need recording. No printout is produced.

To record a batch customer invoice do the following:

If you know the first character of the customer A/C, enter it and choose the Finder button to automatically bring up the first code beginning with this character.

Where you only know the gross value of an invoice, enter it in the Net box and use the Calculate Net button to work out the correct Net value and VAT due.

Always check that the correct Tax Code is used. See page 12.

1 Choose Invoice from the Customers toolbar.

2 Enter the customer Account Code or use the finder button to display a list of codes.

3 Change invoice date if different from current system date.

4 Enter the Invoice Number here and a Reference Number, if required.

5 Change Nominal Code or Department if different from defaults.

6 Enter Net value of invoice here.

7 Click Save to update the nominal ledger and customer details (details posted), then Close.

A/C	Date	Inv No.	Refn	N/C	Dept	Details	Net	T/C	VAT
FEL01	25/10/1999			4000	0		0.00	T1	0.00

A/C Name: Palmer Energy Ltd
N/C Name: Sales Type A
Tax Rate: 17.50
Batch Total: 0.00

Save | Abandon | Calculate Net | Close

Batch Customer Credit Note

A credit note is used, for example, where an error is made and a customer has been overcharged on an invoice, Sometimes, damaged goods are returned and so a credit note is issued showing the amount due to the customer.

Like batch invoicing, credit notes processed manually need entering. To record batch credit notes:

To check the credit note has been posted, make a note of the balance for the appropriate customer in the Customers window before entering the credit note, then check that the balance has reduced by the correct amount after performing Step 6.

1 Click Credit from the Customers toolbar to bring up the Batch Customer Credits window.

2 Enter the customer Account Code.

3 The screen displays the defaults for the nominal account code posting, VAT rate to be applied & department.

		Credits										
A/C Name	Business Exhibitions								Tax Rate			17.50
N/C Name	Sales North East								Batch Total			0.00

A/C	Date	Cd. No	Refn	N/C	Dept	Details	Net	T/C	VAT
BUS001	27/10/1999			4000	1		0.00	T1	0.00
								0.00	0.00

Save	Abandon	Calculate Net		Close

If you need a printout of a credit, generate a product or service credit note from Invoicing on the Sage Line 50 toolbar and the details will be recorded automatically.

4 Enter credit details for each customer in the same way as for batch invoice.

5 Check all values are correct & click Save to post the details or Abandon to start again.

6 Click Close to return to the Customers window.

Debtors Analysis

To identify debtors and monitor cashflow, customers' outstanding balances and transactions need to be regularly checked. These transactions are grouped by the age of the debt, either on calendar months or based on a period of days, e.g. 30, 60 and 90 days etc. Debt chasing letters can be issued if required. Some businesses may use this information to calculate interest charges for late payment.

Use Customer Defaults from the Settings menu to change the age of the debt between calendar months and period of days.

1 From the Customers window select the required customer.

2 Click Aged to bring up the Aged Balances Date Defaults box.

3 Enter the date to be used for calculating the aged balances.

4 To include payments only up to a particular date, enter that date here.

When viewing aged balances in graphical format use the Options facility to select what information you wish to view in the graph.

6 To see the aged balances in graphical format use the Graph tab.

5 Click OK to bring up the Aged Balances window.

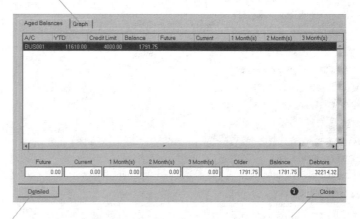

7 For a transaction breakdown click on Detailed.

8 Click Close to return.

Credit Charges

Interest rates applied to credit charges are set using the Finance Rates option from the Settings menu.

Use the Memo box to keep notes on a credit agreement negotiated with the selected customer.

From November 1998 credit charges can be applied for customers whose payments are overdue. To apply this, from the Customers window click Charges to run the Credit Charges Wizard, then follow the instructions.

Before you can use the Wizard, finance rates must have first been set up.

A payment which is 30 days overdue is regarded, by default, as late. If you need to change payment terms, do the following:

1 From the Sage Line 50 toolbar choose the Customers button.

2 Highlight the appropriate customer or customers, then click the Record button.

3 Click on the Credit Control tab to bring up the Credit Control details box.

4 Enter new details in Pay Due Days.

Details	Defaults	Credit Control	Sales	Graphs	Activity	Contacts	Memo

Terms

		Credit Review	
Credit Limit	4000.00	A/C Opened	26/11/1994
Sett. Due Days	0	Last Credit Review	
Sett. Discount	0.00	Next Credit Review	
Pay Due Days	0	Application Date	
Terms	Proforma	Date Received	
Credit Ref.		Memo:	
Bureau			

Restrictions

☐ Can charge credit   ☐ Restrict mailing
☑ Terms agreed   ☑ Account On Hold

Save	Abandon	Delete	Back	Next		Close

5 Apply account restrictions here if desired, such as placing account on hold, allowing credit to be charged etc.

6 Change any of the other terms as required, then click Save.

7 Click Close to return to the Customers window, then Close again.

Disputed Invoices

There may be times when an invoice is questioned by the customer, so until an agreement is made the invoice can be marked as disputed. This option also applies to any invoices not fully paid. Once the problem is resolved, you can remove the disputed flag (indicator). To mark an invoice as disputed:

1 Click on the Dispute button in the Customers window to bring up the Disputed Items window.

Don't forget that you can always use the Finder button to locate the A/C from a drop-down list.

2 Enter the Customer Account Code here and press the Tab key.

3 Click on the transaction you want to mark as disputed.

Use the Dispute button to mark or unmark an invoice as disputed.

	Disputed Items						_ □ ×
Details							

	A/C	BUS001		Name	Business Exhibitions		

Tp	Date	Ref	Details	Tc	Amount	D
SI	15/05/1998	8566	Training	T1	1762.50	d
SI	30/07/1998			T1	129.25	

Save	Abandon	Dispute	Close

4 Click Dispute.

5 Note that the transaction is now marked as 'd'.

6 Click Save to record the transaction.

7 Click Close to return to the Customers window, then Close again.

Customer Reports and Phone

The arrows on the Customers toolbar let you scroll across all available buttons.

Sage Line 50 provides you with a wide range of ready-designed customer reports to suit the majority of needs. To print or view a customer report, do the following:

1 Click on the Reports button in the Customers window.

2 Select the report you require from the Customer Reports list.

Also use this report window to create, edit or delete Customer Reports.

3 Select Printer or Preview.

4 Click Run to generate the report.

An additional Criteria box may appear for some reports for you to enter ranges, such as Customer Reference etc.

5 After printing Close each window.

Phone
Before the Phone button can be used, Sage Line 50 needs to be told which communications port the modem is using.

If your computer modem & telephone share the same line you can ring a customer using the Phone button from the Customers toolbar, then pick up your phone to talk to them.

1 From the Tools menu choose Options and select the Environment tab.

2 Using the FI I key, find the Com port used by the modem and enter it here.

3 Enter a delay in seconds before the modem will dial.

4 Click OK.

Customer Letters and Labels

Remember to select a customer from the list before clicking the Letters button.

Occasionally you may have a need to send standard information to a customer, such as change of address, or to chase up an overdue payment. All of the necessary information needed for these letters is taken from your records.

A number of the more common standard letters are provided with Sage Line 50, but alternatively there is also the option to create new ones. The new letters can be stored for future use.

To send the same letter (e.g., change of address) to all your customers, first deselect all customers using the Clear button in the Customers window before carrying out Steps 2–7.

1 From the Customers window, select the customer or customers you want to send a letter to.

2 Click the Letters button on the Customers toolbar to bring up the Customer Letters list.

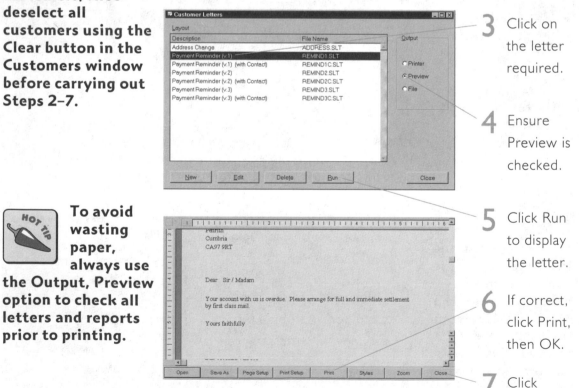

3 Click on the letter required.

4 Ensure Preview is checked.

5 Click Run to display the letter.

6 If correct, click Print, then OK.

7 Click Close.

To avoid wasting paper, always use the Output, Preview option to check all letters and reports prior to printing.

...cont'd

Use the Zoom button if you need to decrease or increase the amount of the page on view. This option lets you zoom in on labels so you can check if they are correct, or to view them as laid out on the page. Note that whilst this is not the same as changing the size of the document window it does have a similar effect.

Labels

To help speed up the process of sending correspondence to customers, use the standard layout label files to print out their names and addresses on predefined labels, or alternatively, create your own.

You have the option as to what data is printed on the label and how the labels are positioned on a page.

1 From the Customers window, select the customer or customers you want to print labels for.

2 Click the Labels button on the Customers toolbar to bring up the Customer Labels list.

3 Click on the label type required.

4 Ensure Preview is checked.

To produce labels for all your customers in one go, make sure no customers are selected in Step 1 by pressing the Clear button, then carry out Steps 2–7.

5 Click Run to produce and display the labels.

6 If correct click Print, then OK.

7 Click Close, then close each window.

The Customer Statement

To keep customers up to date about their financial position, customer statements should be sent out on a regular basis, normally once a month. The statement shows details of all recorded customer transactions, together with a balance figure.

You can also use the Customer Statement window to delete statements no longer required, or to modify and design your own statements.

1 From the Customers window click on the Statements button to bring up the Customer Statements window.

2 Choose the statement layout you require.

3 Ensure Preview is checked.

4 Click Run to bring up the Criteria box.

If you need a copy of the statement saving on disk use the Save As button in the statement preview window and give the statement a file name. You can then open and print the statement at a later date, if required.

5 Enter Customer Reference range.

6 Enter Transaction Date From & To.

7 Click OK to preview statement.

8 Use the Zoom button on the preview to zoom in or out if you need to check any statement details.

9 When satisfied, click Print to print the statement, then Close all windows.

The Supplier Ledger

This chapter shows you how to create and maintain supplier records within the Suppliers (Purchase) Ledger. Through recording invoices and credit notes you receive you can see how much you owe, when these payments are due and any disputed items. You will learn how to view details of any invoices received and payments made to suppliers using tables, graphs and reports.

Covers

The Supplier Toolbar | 34

Creating Supplier Records | 35

Using Criteria | 36

Supplier Activity | 37

Supplier Aged Balance | 38

Recording Supplier Invoices | 39

Recording Supplier Credit Notes | 40

Supplier Letters and Labels | 41

Supplier Reports | 42

Chapter Three

The Supplier Toolbar

The Supplier toolbar has many similar buttons to the Customer toolbar, and again provides you with facilities for setting up records, checking supplier activity, recording invoices, credit notes and reporting.

 Creates a new Supplier Record.

 Opens a Supplier Record.

 View Supplier Activity.

 View Supplier Aged Balances.

 Record Supplier Invoices.

 Record Supplier Credit Notes.

 Opens the Disputed Items window.

 Opens the Credit Charges window.

 To Automatically Dial a Supplier.

 To Print Supplier Labels.

 To Print Standard Letters to Suppliers.

 To Print Supplier Statements.

 To Run Customer Reports.

Creating Supplier Records

Within this window you can view, edit or delete a supplier record. A new supplier record can also be added if you have all of the details to hand. To add a new supplier first select Suppliers from the Sage Line 50 toolbar, then do the following:

Until you are familiar with Sage Line 50, use the New wizard for simple step by step instructions for entering a new supplier record.

1 Click on Record to bring up the Supplier Record window.

2 Use Details to enter supplier information, such as name, address and contact details.

3 Use the O/B button to enter an Opening Balance where required.

Always start with the A/C when entering a new record.

To help save time later, enter accurately as much detail into the record as possible.

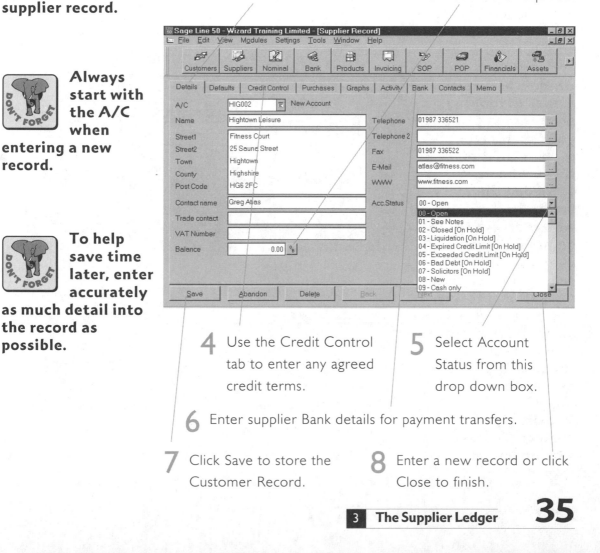

4 Use the Credit Control tab to enter any agreed credit terms.

5 Select Account Status from this drop down box.

6 Enter supplier Bank details for payment transfers.

7 Click Save to store the Customer Record.

8 Enter a new record or click Close to finish.

Using Criteria

This useful Criteria feature is also available within other program windows, such as Customers, Products, Nominal and Invoicing etc.

Use Criteria from the Customers window as a quick means of looking something up about your customers, such as a list of those who have exceeded their credit limit, or whose accounts are on hold. You can even use Criteria to search for a supplier or customer if, say, you only have a single item of detail to hand, such as a telephone number or department, provided this information has been entered when setting up the record.

The Criteria function available within the suppliers window can help save you valuable time when searching for specific information regarding supplier transactions. The following example shows you how to produce a list of suppliers you owe money to:

1 Click the Criteria button in the bottom left hand corner of the Suppliers window to bring up the Criteria window.

2 Click on the Amounts tab.

3 Tick the Balance check box.

4 Select 'Greater than' from the Criteria drop down list.

5 Enter 0 (zero) here.

Criteria				
Details Amounts				
Field		Criteria	Values	
MTD	□	Equal to ▼	0.00	0.00
YTD	□	Equal to ▼	0.00	0.00
Credit Limit	□	Equal to ▼	0.00	0.00
Balance	☑	Greater than ▼	0.00	0.00
Balance Future	□	Equal to ▼	0.00	0.00
Balance Current	□	Equal to ▼	0.00	0.00
1 Month(s)	□	Equal to ▼	0.00	0.00
2 Month(s)	□	Equal to ▼	0.00	0.00
3 Month(s)	□	Equal to ▼	0.00	0.00
Balance (Older)	□	Equal to ▼	0.00	0.00
Over credit limit	□			

Criteria On ☑ ❼   Save   Load   Abandon   Delete   Close

6 Tick the Criteria On check box.

7 Click Close to return to the Suppliers window.

8 Note that the Criteria button is now highlighted and the only records displayed are those that match the given criteria.

9 To cancel the criteria function repeat Steps 6 & 7, this time removing the tick.

Supplier Activity

To view this screen from the Supplier Record window, enter the A/C for the supplier required (if none selected) and then click on the Activity tab.

This feature enables you to view each supplier's transactions in detail. If less complete information is required, you can define a transaction or date range to limit the view:

| From the Suppliers window, click on the supplier you want to look at.

Use the Tidy button to clear all transaction sub-items from view.

2 Click on Activity.

3 In the next box enter the transaction and/or date ranges.

These codes identify the transaction type:

PI = Purchase Invoice.

PP = Purchase Payment.

PC = Purchase Credit Note.

PD = Discount on a Purchase Payment.

PA = Purchase Payment on Account.

4 Click OK to bring up the Activity window.

5 Double-click a transaction for more details.

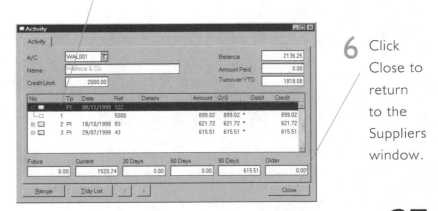

6 Click Close to return to the Suppliers window.

Supplier Aged Balance

The age period is set through Supplier Defaults from the Settings menu. You can base it on either calendar months or a period of days, specified by you. Remember also that ageing is relative to the program date.

Aged balance is the term given to the time lapse of outstanding debt, whether owed *to* or *by* you. Sage Line 50 lets you view the amount of money you owe your Suppliers, grouped on the age of the debt. It is common practice for businesses to give 30 days credit, but others terms are sometimes negotiated. Sage Line 50 default aged periods are 30, 60 and 90 days.

1 From the Suppliers window, click on the supplier you require and select the Aged button from the toolbar.

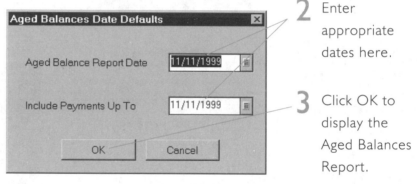

2 Enter appropriate dates here.

3 Click OK to display the Aged Balances Report.

If you need to enter a date only a few days either side of that displayed simply use the cursor up or down keys on the keyboard.

From November 1998 legislation took effect that enables small businesses (less than 50 employees) to charge interest on late payments from large businesses.

4 To see the transactions which make up the aged balance click Detailed.

5 Close each window when finished.

Recording Supplier Invoices

Always check the correct tax code has been selected for the VAT to avoid errors later. Sage Line 50 enters T1 (standard rate) for you by default. You may need to change this to T0 for transactions which are zero rated or to T9 for those not involving VAT.

As with a customer, if you are in dispute with a supplier over an invoice, you can mark it as disputed. See page 28.

'Posting' means updating the Nominal ledger and relevant supplier's details. If you do not wish to save this batch, choose the Abandon button to clear the data and start again.

Invoices received from your suppliers can be entered a few at a time using the Batch Supplier Invoices window. You have full flexibility using this option, such as posting each invoice item to a different nominal account if need be, or allocating to a different VAT code, such as from default VAT to zero VAT. To enter invoices, do the following:

1 From the Suppliers window click Invoice to bring up the Batch Supplier Invoices window.

2 Type the supplier's account code here or use the Finder button.

3 Enter the Date and other invoice details, then check the Nominal (N/C) and Tax (T/C) codes and amend if necessary.

4 When all details are correct and all invoices have been entered, click Save to post the details.

5 Click Close to return to the Suppliers window.

6 Note that the Supplier's record now displays the new balance, then click Close again.

Recording Supplier Credit Notes

Occasionally goods ordered from suppliers may arrive damaged or incomplete. The supplier issues you a credit note reducing the amount owed. Credit notes are recorded using the Credit option from the Suppliers window.

If a credit note contains a number of items, for your benefit it is advisable to enter each transaction individually, but giving them the same account code, date and reference. Sage Line 50 will group these together and list them as a single credit note. You can then view the note in detail using Activity from the Suppliers window.

To see if there is more detail to an entry, just double-click on that entry line.

It is always advisable to check the changes you have made by noting the before and after outstanding balance. This will save time later should a mistake have been made.

It is useful to enter the invoice number that the credit note refers to in the Reference (Refn) box for identification. This will appear in the details under Financials.

1 To record a credit note, from the Suppliers window click Credit.

2 Enter the supplier Account Code. Use the Finder button if you don't have the code.

3 Enter the credit note date.

Batch Supplier Credits

| A/C Name | Wallace & Co. | | | | Tax Rate | | 17.50 |
| N/C Name | Materials Purchased | | | | Batch Total | | 2264.52 |

A/C	Date	Cd. No	Refn	N/C	Dept	Details	Net	T/C	VAT
WAL001	14/11/1999	2564	1655	5000	0	Returned Go	1927.25	T1	337.27
							1927.25		337.27

Save Abandon Calculate Net Close

4 Enter the remaining details and check that they are correct.

5 Click Save to update the nominal ledger and record the credit details.

6 Click Close to return to the Suppliers window.

7 Note that the outstanding balance has changed and click Close.

A/C	Name	Balance	Crd Limit	Contact
HIG002	Hightown Leisure	377.18	1000.00	Greg Atlas
WAL001	Wallace & Co.	1321.68	2000.00	A Wallace

Criteria Swap Clear Delete Close

Supplier Letters and Labels

As with Customers, Sage Line 50 includes the facility to produce preformatted letters and labels for your suppliers. You can create whatever standard letters or label layouts you wish. All the necessary address information etc. is taken from the stored supplier details.

To produce letters or labels for certain suppliers only, click on those suppliers to select them in the Suppliers window before carrying out Steps 1–5. If, however, you want to print letters or labels for all your suppliers, ensure none are selected by clicking on the Clear button in the Suppliers window.

To produce the standard letter informing suppliers of your change of address, do the following:

1 From the Suppliers window click Letters to bring up the Supplier Letters window.

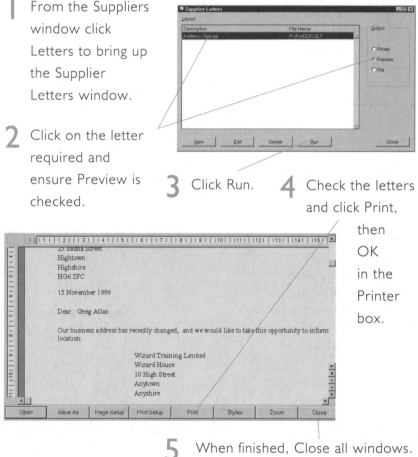

2 Click on the letter required and ensure Preview is checked.

3 Click Run.

4 Check the letters and click Print, then OK in the Printer box.

5 When finished, Close all windows.

Always remember to check that the correct paper, labels and printer type have been selected before printing if you want to avoid wasting time and paper.

Labels

To produce address labels for your suppliers, select the Labels button from the Suppliers window then carry out Steps 2–5 as above.

Supplier Reports

Use the arrow button on the Suppliers toolbar to scroll across to the Reports button.

You can generate a wide range of detailed reports about your suppliers. These reports are produced from the information you entered about suppliers and their transactions. Whilst Sage Line 50 already has a considerable number of reports set up, if any further reports are required you can create them using the Report Designer (see Chapter Twelve). To run or view a supplier report:

A Criteria box will appear when you click Run on most reports for you to enter ranges, such as Supplier Reference, Transaction Date etc.

I Click on the Reports button in the Suppliers window.

2 Select the report you require from the Supplier Reports list.

3 Select Printer or Preview.

4 Click Run to generate the report.

From the Supplier Reports window you can also edit or delete an existing report or create a new one.

If you want to use the phone facility, you must select a Supplier before clicking the Phone button.

5 If a Criteria box appears, enter the From and To details, then click OK.

6 After printing, Close all windows.

The Nominal Ledger

This chapter explains the important role played by the Nominal Ledger and how its accounts detail the flow of money in and out of the business. You will be shown how to analyse these account transactions using tables, graphs and transaction activity reports so you can control and monitor finances through making informed business decisions. You can even tailor your own Nominal Ledger set of accounts to meet specific business needs.

Covers

The Nominal Toolbar | **44**

The Nominal Ledger | **45**

Nominal Records | **46**

Viewing Nominal Transactions | **47**

The Journal | **50**

Making a Journal Entry | **51**

Setting up Prepayments | **52**

Setting up Accruals | **53**

The Chart of Accounts | **54**

Nominal Reports | **56**

Chapter Four

The Nominal Toolbar

The Nominal toolbar buttons provide you with facilities for setting up records, viewing account activity, making journal entries, setting up prepayments and accruals, working on the chart of accounts and reporting.

 Creates a new Nominal Account.

 Opens a Nominal Record.

 View a Nominal Account's Activity.

 Enter Journal double-entries.

 Enter Nominal Ledger Prepayment.

 Enter Nominal Ledger Accrual.

 Opens the Chart of Accounts.

 To Run Nominal Ledger Reports.

The Nominal Ledger

To create a new nominal account, click the New button from the Nominal window.

Click on a record to select or to deselect it. Use the Clear button to deselect all selected records.

Standard nominal accounts for Sage Line 50 are:

- Asset Accounts from 0001 to 1999
- Liability Accounts from 2000 to 3999
- Income Accounts from 4000 to 4999
- Purchase Accounts from 5000 to 5999
- Direct Expenses from 6000 to 6999
- Overheads from 7000 to 9999.

The Nominal Ledger, also referred to as the General Ledger, is a grouped analysis of your sales and purchase transactions. For example, when a sales or purchase invoice is posted to the sales or purchase ledger, Sage Line 50 records it in the Nominal Ledger against the appropriate Nominal account number.

It therefore contains all the accounts for your business, e.g., sales, purchases, expenses, VAT, cash and bank, sundry income, fixed assets, liabilities, capital and owner's drawings, etc. However, it does not keep details of debtors and creditors. These are held in the respective sales and purchase ledgers.

The Nominal accounts let you see quickly where your money is. Information from here is used in the production of management reports to tell you how your business is performing.

N/C	Name	Debit	Credit
0010	Freehold Property		
0011	Leasehold Property		
0020	Plant and Machinery	50000.00	
0021	Plant/Machinery Depreciation		3485.00
0030	Office Equipment		
0031	Office Equipment Depreciation		
0040	Furniture and Fixtures	16900.00	
0041	Furniture/Fixture Depreciation		93.00
0050	Motor Vehicles	20300.00	

1 Click Nominal from the Sage Line 50 toolbar to view the Nominal Ledger.

2 Use scroll bar to view range of accounts.

3 Click Close when finished.

In Sage Line 50, a standard set of nominal accounts are created upon installation, unless in the Startup Wizard you decided to create your own nominal structure. Note that the latter option only creates the Control Accounts for you.

Nominal Records

Check your business performance by initially entering monthly budget and prior year values, then regularly comparing these against the actual value.

You can tailor the nominal accounts to exactly meet your needs by using the Nominal Record window. You have the facility to add, edit and delete nominal accounts as well as viewing transactions posted to each account on a monthly basis.

Using the Record window you can also set budget values for each month of your financial year for a particular nominal account. You can also compare the actual monthly figures against the budget values to keep track of how close you are to meeting targets. To add a nominal account record, do the following:

You can edit a Nominal Account to suit your needs. Simply use the Finder button for Step 2 to locate the N/C, then type any changes in the Details box and click on the Save button.

1 Click Record from the Nominal Ledger to bring up the Nominal Record window.

2 In the Details tab box, enter the new nominal account code here.

Nominal Record

Details	Graphs	Activity	Memo

N/C `4004` New Account

Name `Sales North West`

Balance `0.00` Account Type

Month	Actuals	Budgets	Prior Yr
B/F	0.00	0.00	0.00
Jan	0.00	5000.00	4000.00
Feb	0.00	4300.00	3800.00
Mar	0.00	700.00	650.00
Apr	0.00	3200.00	2250.00
May	0.00	1000.00	600.00
Jun	0.00	1000.00	600.00
Jul	0.00	4300.00	3700.00

Save	Abandon	Delete	Back	Next	Close

The New account details must first be saved before an Opening Balance can be entered.

3 Press the Tab key and note that this is a New Account.

4 Enter new account Name, Budget and Prior Year values.

5 Click Save to store details or Abandon to start again.

6 Click Close to return to the Nominal Ledger.

Viewing Nominal Transactions

You can view your Nominal Ledger transactions by using:

- Graphs.

- Activity reports.

- Table formats.

Transaction Analysis using Graphs

A range of 2D and 3D charts is available in Sage Line 50 to visually compare your current year's trading against the previous year and any budgets you have put in place.

 You can save the graph to disk as a chart file. Click on Disk icon and enter a file name.

 Use this button to switch between 2D and 3D graph.

 You can change what you view on the graph by clicking on the Options button and altering the View or Compare selection.

1 From the Nominal Ledger window, select the nominal account you wish to view.

2 Click Record, then select the Graphs tab to display data in graphical form.

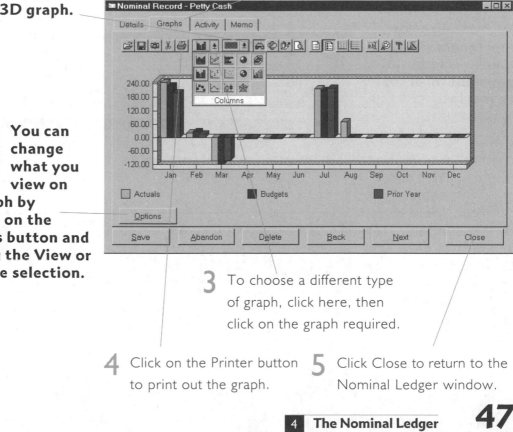

3 To choose a different type of graph, click here, then click on the graph required.

4 Click on the Printer button to print out the graph.

5 Click Close to return to the Nominal Ledger window.

Viewing Nominal Account Activity

You will occasionally need to view transactions that have been posted to the nominal ledger accounts. To do this from the Nominal Ledger window:

Transactions already cleared from the audit trail are shown as a single carried forward total and displayed as an Opening Balance (O/BAL).

1 Click on the nominal account you wish to view.

2 Click on the Activity button to bring up the Defaults box.

3 Enter the appropriate Transaction and Date ranges.

4 Click OK to display Activity.

Each line of the Activity list box represents a single invoice, credit note, payment on account or receipt.

No		Tp	Date	Ref.	Details	Amount	Debit	Credit
			01/01/1999		B/Fwd Balance	797.15		797.15
		CP	15/11/1999	2256				
	694			7300	Petrol	11.75		11.75
	695	SR	15/11/1999	Cash	Sales Receipt	1228.56	1228.56	
	719	SR	30/11/1999		Sales Receipt	70.24	70.24	
	781	CP	03/12/1999	Cash	Faxes	1.50		1.50

1298.80 810.40
488.40

You can select more than one account to view at a time and simply use the '<' and '>' arrow buttons to scroll through them.

5 Double-click a transaction to view any further details.

6 Use the arrow buttons to view other nominal accounts, if more than one is selected in Step 1.

7 Click Close to return to the Nominal Ledger.

...cont'd

Transaction Codes

Transactions in the Activity window are identified by a type (Tp) or transaction code, allocated by Sage Line 50. The following is a list of transaction codes used:

The Ref. column in the Activity window shows the reference given to the transaction when it was posted.

BR (Bank Receipt)	SD (Discount on Sales Receipt)
BP (Bank Payment)	SA (Sales Receipt on Account)
CP (Cash Payment)	PI (Purchase Invoice)
CR (Cash Receipt)	PP (Purchase Payment)
JD (Journal Debit)	PC (Purchase Credit)
JC (Journal Credit)	PD (Discount on Purchase Payment)
SI (Sales Invoice)	PA (Purchase Payment on Account)
SR (Sales Receipt)	VP (Visa Credit Payments)
SC (Sales Credit)	VR (Visa Credit Receipts)

Using Criteria

You can tell at a glance if criteria is being applied to a list because the text on the Criteria button will be bold.

It is sometimes handy to reduce the number of records displayed in the Nominal Ledger window or on your reports to only those that match a specific criteria. This will save you having to search through too many records just to find the information you need. For example, this is how to list only control accounts in the Nominal Ledger window:

1 Click Criteria in the Nominal Ledger window.

2 Tick Account type.

3 Select Equal to and Control Account here.

Criteria remains applied to a list until the tick entered in Step 4 is removed. Performing Steps 1, 4 & 5 will do this for you.

4 Tick Criteria On.

5 Click Close to action.

The Journal

The rules for debits and credits are: Debit the account which receives the value; Credit the account which gives the value.

The Journal allows you to make transfers between any of your nominal account codes regardless of type (Asset, Liability, Income or Expenditure), provided you adhere to double-entry bookkeeping principles. It lets you enter transactions which may not be covered within the standard Sage Line 50 facilities.

It is a useful source of reference for these non-regular transactions and can reduce errors by providing a list (audit trail) for checking purposes. Examples of these transactions include correction of errors and transfer of monies, as well as the purchase and sale of fixed assets on credit.

If you use the journal to record transfer of monthly salary payments, use the Monthly Salary skeleton journal provided by Sage Line 50.

As stated, the Journal follows double-entry bookkeeping principles, i.e., the value of the credit transaction must equal the value of the debit transaction. Each line of the Journal Entry table represents a single transaction; therefore there must be at least two transactions in the journal (a credit and a debit).

However, this does not mean that you must post a single credit item for every single debit item. You can, for example, post several debits but only one balancing credit, and vice versa. Provided the net difference between your postings is always zero (i.e. the total value of credits equals the total value of debits), you can then post the Journal.

'Skeleton' Journals

For journals that you make regularly, payments from a bank to a credit card account for example, Sage Line 50 lets you save the details of that journal entry so that you can use it the next time without having to enter it all again. This is called a 'skeleton'. Some skeleton journals were set up at installation, such as the VAT Liability Transfer Journal.

For details about the skeleton journals set up for you in Sage Line 50, see the Library Help and Search for Skeleton.

To save a skeleton journal, click on the Memorise button after you have set up the journal. To load a skeleton journal, click on the Recall button, select the journal you need and click on the Load button.

You can even load one of the skeleton journals provided by Sage Line 50, modify it to suit your needs, then save it.

Making a Journal Entry

For a journal entry, VAT is neither calculated for you nor posted to the VAT control account.

Here is an example of how you would make a journal entry for a transfer of funds between your business building society account and bank account.

1 From the Nominal Ledger toolbar, click Journal.

2 Use the Calendar button if a different date is required.

If you use a journal entry regularly save it as a Skeleton using the Memorise button, so you can re-create it quickly and easily later.

Nominal Ledger Journals

Journals

Ref	Date					Balance
TRANS	19/11/1999					0.00

N/C	Name	Dept	Details	Tc	Debit	Credit
1210	Bank Deposit Account	0	Transfer	T9	0.00	450.00
1220	Building Society Account	0	Transfer	T9	450.00	0.00
					450.00	450.00

Save   Abandon   Memorise   Recall   Close

3 Enter details for both the credit and debit transactions. The Ref. entry is optional.

4 Note, the default Tax code of T9 is entered for you by Sage Line 50.

5 Check total Debit and Credit are equal and a zero balance is displayed in the Balance box.

6 Click Save to process your journal or Abandon to cancel.

7 Click Close to return to Nominal Ledger window.

Before saving the Journal, always ensure the Balance box shows zero. If the value of the credit transactions does not equal the value of the debit transactions, then Sage Line 50 issues a warning and will not let you save the Journal.

Note that Sage Line 50 will not automatically calculate VAT, or post it to the VAT Control Account. If VAT is required, enter each VAT element as a separate line, with a debit or credit to the appropriate VAT Control Account.

Setting up Prepayments

Just click on the Wizard Button in the Prepayments window to let the Prepayments Wizard guide you through setting up a prepayment.

To adjust statements and reports for any payments which have to be made in advance, for example rent or insurance, there is a Prepayments option available from the Nominal Ledger window. This allows for a payment to be shown as spread over the number of months it refers to, not just the month it was paid in.

After setting up a prepayment, when you run the Month End procedure the correct monthly figure is posted to the appropriate account. All you have to do is to remember to post a suitable payment for the full amount (i.e. from the bank) to the appropriate nominal account.

Use Key F6 to save time and reduce errors when copying data from a previous transaction row.

You will need to post a payment to the Prepayments account for the full amount.

No accounting takes place when prepayment details are saved. Journal Entry postings are only made when the Month End, Post Prepayments option is run.

1 From the Nominal Ledger toolbar, click Prepay to bring up the Prepayments window.

2 Enter relevant nominal account code or use the Finder button.

3 Enter a suitable description.

4 Enter total net value of prepayment.

5 Enter number of months this prepayment covers, up to a maximum of twelve.

6 Note that monthly rate is entered for you.

7 Click Save to accept prepayment details.

8 Click Close to return to Nominal Ledger window.

Setting up Accruals

The Post column shows how many postings have been made using the Month End Post prepayment option.

The Accruals option allows the accounts to be adjusted for any payments you make in one accounting period which in fact relate to a previous period, such as a gas or electricity bill.

In this example, the transaction would be entered using the Accrual and Gas or Electricity accounts when the charges actually fall due, but when the bill is paid, the payment transaction is applied to the Accrual account and not the Gas or Electricity account.

As with the prepayments option, the accruals are posted as part of your month end procedure using the Period End, Month End option. This procedure automatically updates the audit trail and nominal accounts records.

You will need to post a payment to the Accruals account for the full amount.

No accounting takes place when accrual details are saved. Journal Entry postings are only made when the Month End, Post Accruals option is run.

2 Enter relevant nominal account code, or use the Finder button.

1 From the Nominal Ledger window click Accrual.

3 Enter accrual details.

4 Enter the estimated total net value of accrual here.

5 Enter number of months for the accrual.

6 Monthly accrual is calculated for you.

7 Click Save to accept accrual details.

8 Click Close to return to Nominal Ledger window.

The Chart of Accounts

 The chart of Accounts is subdivided into the following default report category types:

Profit & Loss
- Sales
- Purchases
- Direct Expenses
- Overheads.

Balance Sheet
- Fixed Assets
- Current Assets
- Current Liabilities
- Long Term Liabilities
- Capital & Reserves.

During installation, Sage Line 50 created a simple Chart of Accounts suitable for standard reporting, such as Profit and Loss, Balance Sheet, Budget and Prior Year Reports.

It may be that the default account names are not suitable for your business, so the Chart of Accounts can be customised to meet your business requirements. New category types can be introduced into the accounts or current categories edited to reflect, for example, the actual items sold within your business.

1 To examine the Chart of Accounts' facilities, click COA from the Nominal Ledger window.

2 If you want to look at a chart, select it from the list and click Edit.

 Every time you run your financial reports, you can select another layout if you wish.

Chart of Accounts

Description
Default Layout of Accounts
Layout 2

Current | Default Layout of Accounts

[Add] [Edit] [Remove] [Current]   [Close]

3 To create a new Chart of Accounts, click the Add button.

4 To use a particular Chart of Accounts simply highlight it from the list and click the Current button.

 Check that the name of the layout you selected appears automatically in the 'Current' text box.

5 When finished, click Close to return to the Nominal Ledger window.

...cont'd

If you elected to create your own chart of accounts during the Startup Wizard, the default chart of accounts will not contain any category accounts.

When you run your financial reports, the value of each nominal account within each category account will be added together.

When entering nominal account ranges in Low/High boxes, type the same number in both boxes if only one code exists.

Use the Check button to find any nominal account errors in your new layout.

Creating a Chart of Accounts Layout

If you need to add a new Chart of Accounts layout, do the following:

1 Click COA from the Nominal Ledger window.

2 Click Add in the Chart of Accounts window.

3 Enter name of your new Chart of Accounts layout.

4 Click Add to continue.

5 Click on a category and change its description to that required in your financial reports.

6 Enter (or amend) the headings for each range of nominal accounts in the selected category.

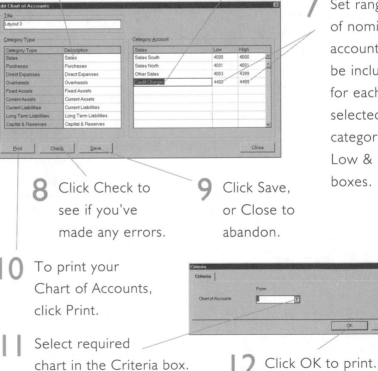

7 Set range of nominal accounts to be included for each selected category in Low & High boxes.

8 Click Check to see if you've made any errors.

9 Click Save, or Close to abandon.

10 To print your Chart of Accounts, click Print.

11 Select required chart in the Criteria box.

12 Click OK to print.

Nominal Reports

Also use the Nominal Reports window to delete a report or if you need to create or edit reports.

To print or preview reports using the nominal data already entered into the system, use the Reports option from the Nominal Ledger. Sage Line 50 already supplies a considerable number of pre-installed reports to suit most needs, but you can create additional custom reports using the Report Designer. See Chapter 12 for more details on creating reports.

To print a Nominal Ledger report, do the following:

1 From the Nominal Ledger toolbar, click Reports.

Use the Criteria button on the Nominal Ledger window to make report generation easier by restricting the selection of nominal account codes to specified criteria.

2 Click on report layout required.

3 Check Output is set to Preview.

4 Click Run to bring up the Criteria box.

5 Type range details or use the Calendar and Finder buttons.

You may sometimes find it easier to select nominal accounts from the Nominal Ledger window instead of entering them in the Criteria box.

6 Click OK to preview report.

7 If a printout is required, click on the Print button.

8 Click Close to return to the Layout window.

9 Close all windows to finish.

The Bank

This chapter shows you how to maintain your bank account records and transactions. This includes deposits, payments, transfer of money between bank accounts and adjustments to show bank charges and interest received. It also covers reconciling your statements, processing recurring entries and a new facility, the automatic production of cheques.

Covers

The Bank Toolbar | 58

Bank Accounts | 59

Bank, Cash and Credit Card Accounts | 60

Recording Bank Payments | 61

Supplier Invoice Payments | 62

Batch Purchase Payments | 63

Bank Receipts | 64

Recording Customer Receipts | 65

Bank Transfers | 66

Recurring Entries | 67

Generating Cheques | 68

The Bank Statement | 69

Bank Account Reconciliation | 70

Bank Reports | 72

Chapter Five

The Bank Toolbar

This toolbar provides features for the recording and maintenance of bank transactions and records. You can perform adjustments, record the transfer of monies, enter receipts, produce statements and reports and even print cheques.

 Creates a new Bank Account.

 Opens a Bank Record.

 Opens Bank Account Reconciliation.

 Record Bank Payments.

 Record Supplier Payments.

 Record a Batch Purchase Payment.

 Record Money Received.

 Record Customer receipts.

 Make Bank Transfers.

 Opens Recurring Entries Window.

 To Print Bank Statements.

 To Print Cheques.

 To Run Bank Account Reports.

Bank Accounts

To guide you through creating a new Bank account, use the New Wizard from the Bank Toolbar.

There are three types of Bank accounts used in Sage Line 50: the Bank Account, Cash Account and Credit Card Account.

The Bank account option treats both Bank and Building Societies as bank accounts. Three bank accounts have been automatically set up to include a bank current account, a bank deposit account and a building society account.

A single Cash Account called Petty Cash has been set up, but other cash accounts can be added, for example, Emergency Cash or Additional Travel Expenses etc.

The arrows on the Customers toolbar let you scroll across all available buttons.

The facility to record your credit card bank details is available and allows you to monitor any credit card transactions you have made and keep track of your money. Two credit card accounts have already been set up for use.

To view the Bank account window:

1 From the Sage Line 50 Toolbar click on the Bank icon.

Have your current bank balance to hand when creating new Bank records.

Sage Line 50 treats both Bank and Building Societies as Bank accounts.

2 Click once on the bank account required, then click on the appropriate icon for the function you wish to carry out.

3 When finished, click Close.

Bank, Cash and Credit Accounts

Use the Bank Record Wizard to guide you through setting up a new bank account.

Sage Line 50 provides three types of bank accounts:

- Bank Account (includes both bank deposit and current account, plus a building society account).

- Cash Account (named Petty Cash).

- Credit Card Account (company credit card and credit card receipts).

Refer to Chapter Thirteen for more information on entering opening balances.

These accounts can be edited to match your own details. Accounts can also be added or deleted. To set up your Bank account details:

1 From the Bank Accounts window, select account type required and click on the Record icon.

2 Make changes if necessary here.

Your bank accounts and financial reports use nominal codes 1200 to 1299.

3 Click here to enter Current Balance. The Opening Balance Setup box appears.

4 Enter Opening Balance and other details.

5 Click Save.

6 Click Bank Details tab and enter further details.

Should the minimum balance fall below the figure entered, it will be displayed in red in the Bank Accounts window.

7 Click Save to store details, then Close.

Recording Bank Payments

Any payments to your suppliers should be entered using the Supplier option as this will automatically bring up any outstanding invoices when the supplier's account reference is entered.

For recording any non-invoiced or one-off payments use the Payment option from the Bank Accounts window. Sage Line 50 then makes it very easy for you to keep track of where your money goes – simply select the appropriate account, enter the payment and post it.

To record Bank payments:

1 Click Payment from the Bank Accounts window.

2 Use Finder button to enter Bank account code.

3 Enter Date and transaction Reference (if required).

If you only know the Gross value of the payment, simply enter it in the Net box and click on the Calculate Net button.

Bank Payments								
Bank Payments								
Bank	Bank Current Account					Tax Rate		17.50
N/C Name	Miscellaneous Purchases					Batch Total		147.46
Bank	Date	Ref	N/C	Dept	Details	Net	Tc	Tax
1200	24/11/1999		5002	0	Purchases	125.50	T1	21.96
						125.50		21.96
Save	Abandon	Calculate Net						Close

4 Enter a Nominal Code for the payment to be posted to, or use the Finder button.

5 Enter Details.

6 Enter amount (change Tax Code from default of T1 if necessary).

Use the Abandon button if you want to clear the data and start again. Any entries already saved will not be cancelled.

7 Click Save to post details (update the nominal ledger and the Bank account).

8 Click Close to finish.

Supplier Invoice Payments

A warning appears if you try to pay a disputed invoice. Only when the invoice is paid in full does the disputed flag disappear.

Leave the cheque number blank if you intend using the Cheques option. Cheques will be automatically generated for you.

Enter a discount value in the discount box, not a percentage, for any invoiced item. The Analysis Total box decreases by the discount value entered.

You don't have to enter a value on the cheque: Sage Line 50 does it for you.

The Supplier option from the Bank Accounts toolbar will provide you with a detailed transaction list of any outstanding invoice items, credit notes and payments made on account to suppliers. To record payment of a supplier invoice do the following:

1 From the Bank Accounts window, click on the type of bank account required (e.g., Bank Current Account).

2 Enter supplier account code.

3 Use Calendar button if payment date is different.

Supplier Payment - Bank Current Account

Bank Current Account   Date: 24/11/1999   Chq.No. _____

Payee: WAL001   Wallace & Co.

One thousand, five hundred twenty Pounds and 74p   £   1520.74

Wizard Training Limited

No.	Tp	A/c	Date	Ref	Details	Tc	Amount	d	Payment	Discount
1	PI	WAL001	08/11/1999	122	Flip charts	n/a	899.02		899.02	0.00
2	PI	WAL001	18/10/1999	93	Stationery	n/a	621.72		621.72	0.00
3	PI	WAL001	29/07/1999	43		n/a	615.51		0.00	0.00
4	PI	WAL001	12/11/1999	12345		n/a	1449.95		0.00	0.00

Bank Balance   -1520.74   Analysis Total   1520.74

Save   Abandon   Pay in Full   Remittance   Wizard   Automatic   Dept.   Close

---

5 Enter value in Payment box for part-payment or click on Pay in Full button to enter full amount.

4 Enter cheque number if required. (See the first REMEMBER icon in the margin.)

6 Repeat Step 5 for any remaining transactions.

7 Click Remittance button to print remittance.

8 Click Save to save payment details and Close.

Batch Purchase Payments

You can list all outstanding purchase invoices, purchase credit notes and purchase payments on account for all suppliers using the Batch option from the Bank Accounts window. The transactions are sorted firstly by supplier and then by transaction number.

Outstanding transactions can be paid in three ways:

- All transactions paid in full.

- Individual transactions paid in full.

- Individual transactions paid in part.

To record full or part payments:

You can pay a transaction in full or part.

All outstanding transactions can be paid in full in one go using the Pay All button, but there will only be one posting.

If any transactions are in dispute a warning message appears.

1 From Bank Accounts select the account and click Batch.

2 To pay ALL outstanding transactions click Pay All.

Batch Purchase Payments

Outstanding Transactions

| Bank | Bank. Current Account | | | | | | | Date | 28/11/1999 |
| A/C Name | Wallace & Co. | | | | | | | | |

No.	Tp	A/c	Date	Ref	Details	Tc	Amount	d	Payment	Discount
5	PI	HIG002	14/11/1999	234		n/a	377.18		0.00	0.00
1	PI	WAL001	08/11/1999	122	Flip charts	n/a	899.02		0.00	0.00
2	PI	WAL001	18/10/1999	93	Stationery	n/a	621.72		0.00	0.00
3	PI	WAL001	29/07/1999	43		n/a	615.51		0.00	0.00
4	PI	WAL001	12/11/1999	12345		n/a	1449.95		0.00	0.00
6	PC	WAL001	14/11/1999	2564	Returned Gc	n/a	2264.52		0.00	0.00

| Bank Balance | 0.00 | | | Total | 0.00 |

| Save | Abandon | Pay in Full | Pay All | Department | Close |

Regularly check the values in the Total and Bank Balance boxes.

3 To make INDIVIDUAL full payments, select a transaction and click on the Pay in Full button.

4 For a PART PAYMENT simply enter the amount in the Payment box.

5 When finished, Click Save or Abandon to start again.

6 Click Close.

Bank Receipts

For payment of goods and services by credit card, deposit a batch of credit card vouchers into your Bank account (Company Credit Card Receipts).

To record any non-invoiced or miscellaneous money you receive, the Receipts option from the Bank Accounts window is used. These items are allocated a specific nominal code for analysis purposes so a check can be made on monies received.

To enter receipt of money:

1 From the Bank Account window Click on the Receipt icon.

2 In the Bank Receipts window, select the appropriate Bank account.

3 Ensure the required Date is entered here.

4 Enter a Reference here, such as a cheque number.

If you only have the Gross value to hand, enter it in the Net box and click on Calculate Net.

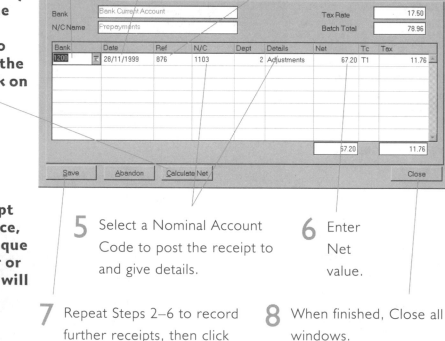

A receipt reference, i.e., cheque number or deposit number, will help when reconciling bank accounts.

5 Select a Nominal Account Code to post the receipt to and give details.

6 Enter Net value.

7 Repeat Steps 2–6 to record further receipts, then click Save to post transactions.

8 When finished, Close all windows.

Recording Customer Receipts

First enter the gross amount received in the Amount box, then check to ensure this equals the Analysis Total when you have finished.

The Customer option from the Bank Accounts window is used to record money received from your customers. When the customer's account reference is entered any outstanding invoices appear automatically in the Customer Receipt window.

To record full payments:

1 From the Bank Accounts window, select the bank account required and click Customer.

Use the Customers Receipt Wizard to help you record invoice payments by cheque, allocate all credit notes and payments on account to invoices or post a payment on account only.

2 Enter a customer Account Code to display all items not fully paid for that customer.

3 Change Date if necessary and enter a paying in Reference if possible.

Customer Receipt - Bank Current Account

A/C	Name	Date	Ref	Amount
PEL01	Palmer Energy Ltd	28/11/1999		0.00

No.	Tp	A/c	Date	Ref	Details	Tc	Amount	d	Receipt	Discount
12	SI	PEL01	28/10/1999	1		n/a	1268.53		0.00	0.00
13	SI	PEL01	15/11/1999	5		n/a	551.08		0.00	0.00

Bank Balance 0.00   Analysis Total 0.00

Save | Abandon | Pay in Full | Wizard | Automatic | Department | Close

You can pay an invoice in full or part but you cannot allocate an amount more than the item value.

4 If FULL payment has been received select a transaction and click Pay in Full.

5 If this is a PART payment enter the amount received here.

Sage Line 50 will automatically warn you of any disputed items.

6 Enter any further receipts then click Save to process them or Abandon to start again.

7 When finished, Close all windows.

Bank Transfers

There is also a Wizard to help you make a Bank Transfer.

Sometimes you will need to transfer money from one bank account to another. You can record this using the Transfer option from the Bank Accounts window or by making a journal entry.

To make a bank transfer do the following:

You can also record a Bank Transfer through a journal entry.

1 From the Bank Accounts window, select the bank you wish to move the money from.

2 Click Transfer to bring up the Bank Transfer window.

The Reference details will be recorded in the audit Trail. You are allowed up to eight characters.

4 Enter a Reference and appropriate Details.

3 Enter Nominal Code of the Bank you are transferring to.

5 Check the correct date is entered in the Date box.

Sage Line 50 always enters today's date in the Date box, but this can be altered if necessary.

6 Enter transfer amount.

7 Click Save to process the transfer or Abandon to start again.

8 Click Close to finish, then Close again.

Recurring Entries

Recurring entries need processing each month before you can run the Month or Year End procedures.

For payments which remain consistent and are paid on a monthly basis, for example rent and electricity, the Recurring option can be used from the Bank Accounts window. This feature is also useful for standing orders and direct debits and prevents payments such as these from being overlooked. Each month, these transactions need posting to update your banks and ledgers.

If there are any outstanding recurring entries, you will be reminded to post them. To add a recurring entry:

Sage Line 50 will only let you post journal credits when you post journal debits of the same value, and vice versa.

1 Select Recurring from the Bank Accounts window and Click Add.

2 Enter transaction type from the list box.

3 Enter the Bank Account Code.

Add / Edit Recurring Entry

Trans. Type	Payment
Bank A/C	1200 Bank Current Account
Nominal Code	0030 Office Equipment
Ref	DD/STO Details
Department	0
Day to post	0
Last Posted	☐ Suspend Posting
Net Amount	45.10 Tax Code T1 17.50 VAT 7.89

OK   Cancel

The Last Posted box will remain blank until the new entry is saved and processed.

4 Enter a Nominal Code to post the transaction to.

5 Give a Reference and Description as required.

To stop a monthly payment, click the Suspend Posting box. This is handy for some payments which do not need posting every month.

6 Enter Net amount and check the Tax Code.

7 Click OK to return to the Recurring Entries window.

8 Click Process and Process All to process the recurring entries, then click Close to finish

Generating Cheques

Use the Date Range check box to generate cheques between specified dates.

This is a new feature within Sage Line 50 and offers the ability to print cheques automatically for a particular bank account. All Purchase Payments (type PP) and Purchase Payments on Account (type PA) transactions not previously printed and with blank references are listed in the Print Cheques window. This is how to print cheques using the cheque generator:

1 From the Bank Accounts window, select the required bank account and click on the Cheques button.

2 Allocate a new Cheque Number if required.

If no transactions are selected, the program will print cheques for ALL the listed transactions.

Sage Line 50 allocates to cheques unique, incrementing cheque numbers. When the cheques have been printed correctly, the next available cheque number is stored within the Bank record.

3 Select transactions requiring cheques.

4 Click Print.

5 Select layout required, then click Run.

6 Click Yes if cheques printed correctly, then Close.

The Bank Statement

Sage Line 50 provides you with the facility to print your bank statements out at any time, showing all reconciled bank payments and receipts.

To use this facility effectively, you should make sure that you enter all Bank transactions accurately and completely so that the Sage Line 50 Bank statements match your actual bank statements.

These statements show the transactions made to and from each bank account, and prove useful for cross-referencing purposes when checking for any transaction omissions or additions. To print a report in bank statement format, do the following:

1 From the Bank Accounts window click on the Statement button to bring up the Criteria window.

2 Enter Transaction Date range.

3 Enter To and From Bank Ref's, using the Finder button for ease.

4 Select Preview from Output options.

You can also save the Bank Statement reports as a file for use at a later date. Simply click on the Save As button in the report preview window.

5 Click Run to preview statement.

To bring up previously saved statements, Click Open and select the required statement from the list.

6 Click Print and OK from the print dialog box.

7 Click Close to return to the Bank Accounts window.

Bank Account Reconciliation

Before you select any transactions to reconcile, always check that the opening balance shown in the Bank Reconciliation window is the same as the opening balance on your actual bank statement.

Refer to the F1 help key or the Library for additional information about bank reconciliation.

A bank account cannot be reconciled if the check box No Bank Reconciliation has been selected on the bank record.

To search for specific transactions, use the Find button.

Bank reconciliation is the process of matching up your computer bank records and transactions with those shown on your bank statements.

The Bank Reconciliation window displays transactions which have not been previously reconciled. After entering the date of the statement, you can work through your bank statement matching the transactions recorded in Sage Line 50. If necessary, you should make any adjustments needed to ensure that Sage Line 50 bank accounts accurately reflect the transactions processed by your actual bank. To reconcile a bank account:

1 From the Bank Accounts window select the bank account to be reconciled, then click Reconcile.

2 Enter the date of the actual bank statement and press Tab.

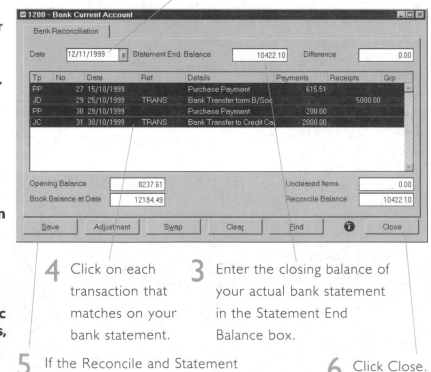

4 Click on each transaction that matches on your bank statement.

3 Enter the closing balance of your actual bank statement in the Statement End Balance box.

5 If the Reconcile and Statement End balances match, click Save.

6 Click Close.

...cont'd

Thoroughly check all transactions on the bank statement against the Bank Reconciliation list. Check that the Reconcile Balance box matches the closing balance of your bank statement.

As you select each transaction you will see the Reconcile Balance change automatically.

Use Adjustments button or Bank Payments, Receipts and Transfers to record any additional transactions shown on your bank statement, e.g., bank charges, cash point withdrawals etc.

Bank reconciliation will only work correctly provided that a number of important rules are followed:

• The opening balance shown on the Bank Reconciliation window must match the opening balance on your actual bank statement.

If for some reason they are different, you will need to check why and make the necessary adjustments. One way of doing this is to view the selected bank's activity from within the nominal ledger. To see if a transaction has been reconciled or not, check the Bank column in the Audit Trail, where R = reconciled and N = not reconciled.

• Work through your actual bank statement progressively one line at a time, clicking on the corresponding transaction entry in the Bank reconciliation window to highlight it.

• If you come across a transaction on your bank statement not shown in Sage Line 50, you should record this transaction immediately using the Adjustments facility.

• Check everything carefully. When you are satisfied that all necessary transactions for reconciliation have been selected and any adjustments made, the Difference box should show zero.

Making Adjustments

1 From the Reconciliation window, click on the Adjustments button.

2 Enter the Nominal Code of the account to receive the adjustment.

3 Enter adjustment details.

4 If correct click Save, then Close.

Bank Reports

When you have become familiar with the various reports you can save time by sending them straight to the printer without the need to preview. Select Printer instead of Preview in Step 3.

There is a wide range of ready-to-use bank reports provided by Sage Line 50. These reports outline your bank details and transactions and help you keep track of your bank finances. It is advisable that you regularly print out the standard reports, such as Day Books, once you have entered the relevant transactions.

1 From the Bank Accounts window, click Reports to bring up the Bank Reports window.

2 Click on the report required.

3 Ensure Preview is selected.

You can save a report as a file in a number of useful formats, such as Microsoft Write, Text file or Comma Separated Value (CSV).

4 Click Run to bring up the Criteria window.

5 Enter Criteria required for report.

If you chose to print the report, the Windows Print dialog box appears. Use this to select which pages to print and change your printer settings if necessary.

6 Click OK to generate the report.

7 Click Print, then OK and Close.

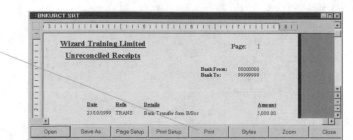

Products

This chapter shows you how to create and maintain records for products you buy and sell and how to set up product codes. These details, once recorded in the system, will be entered automatically for you when creating sales orders, purchase orders and invoices etc. You will learn how to monitor stock levels as well as the movement of stock and analyse product transactions using tables, graphs and reports.

Covers

The Products Toolbar | 74

The Product Record | 75

Product Defaults | 78

Using Criteria | 79

Bill of Materials | 80

Viewing Transactions | 81

Product Activity | 82

Product Adjustments | 84

Product Transfers | 85

Product Reports | 86

Chapter Six

The Products Toolbar

The Products toolbar provides features for the recording and maintenance of product records and transactions. You have the facility to record the movement of your products and make any adjustments and/or transfer of stock. Product activity can be analysed and reports generated.

 Creates a new Product Record.

 Opens a Product Record.

 View a Product Activity.

 Make Stock In Adjustments.

 Make Stock Out Adjustments.

 Record Stock Transfers.

 To Run Product Reports.

The Product Record

Sage Line 50 allows you to divide products into 999 different categories using the Product Categories option from the Settings menu.

Sage Line 50 allows you to create, edit or delete records for all the products your business sells. Once these records have been set up all you need to do is enter a product code and the details will be automatically included for you on any product invoice, credit note or order you create.

From the Product Record window you can view the sales price and quantity in stock for each product. Use the Products option to:

- Create and maintain records for all products bought and sold.

- Record product movements.

- Analyse product transactions using tables or graphs.

- Set up a Bill of Materials.

- Keep track of your stock levels.

Opening Balances need setting up for your products following the same procedures as for your customers, suppliers, nominal and bank accounts.

From the Product Record window you can view the Sales Price and Quantity in stock for each product, together with the Product Code and Description.

1 To bring up the Products window click Products from the Sage Line 50 toolbar.

2 To view Product details, select the product and click Record.

Once a product record has been set up, take care before deleting it, even if there is zero stock and no more is expected. It may still belong to a part allocated order.

Products							
New	Record	Activity	In	Out	Transfer	Reports	

Product Code	Description	Sales Price	Qty
AAA	Automatic Kettle	53.98	39.00
BBB	Waste Bin - Floral	23.45	55.00
CHOC01	Box of Chocolates - 500 gms	12.75	70.00

Criteria	Swap	Clear	Delete	Close

3 To finish click Close.

Header

...cont'd

You may find it easier at first to let the Product Record Wizard create a new product record for you. Just click on the New option from the Products window.

You can update the sales price for all product items using the Global Changes option from the Tools menu. You can increase or decrease the price by a sum or a percentage.

If the Ignore Stock Levels check box is selected (ticked) on the product record, its details will not appear on some reports, i.e., Stock History.

Entering a product record

1 From the Products window click on Record.

2 Type a unique Product Code here and press Tab.

3 Enter Description.

4 Enter relevant details here.

5 Choose a Nominal sales account for this product.

6 Select correct VAT code.

7 Enter Sales Price here.

8 Click on O/B button to bring up the Opening Product Setup box.

9 Check for correct Date.

10 Enter Quantity.

11 Enter Cost Price of Product.

12 Click Save.

13 Enter any remaining details on the Product Record.

14 Click Save to keep the record, or Abandon to abort.

15 Click Close to return to Products window.

Product Record screenshot

Product Record

Details | Memo | BOM | Sales | Graph | Activity | Discount

Product Code: CHOC01
Description: Box of Chocolates - 500 gms
Department: 0
Category: 1
Location:
Com. Code:
Nominal Code: 4000
Supplier A/C:
Sales Price: 12.75
☐ Ignore Stock Levels

Weight: 0.00
Tax Code: T1 17.50
Part No.:
Unit of Sale: 1
Stock Take Date:

In Stock: 70.00
Allocated: 0.00
Free Stock: 70.00
On Order: 0.00
Last Ord Qty: 0.00
Last Ord Date:
Re-order Level: 0.00
Re-order Qty: 0.00
Cost Price: 10.00
Stock Take Qty: 0.00

Save | Abandon | Delete | Back | Next | Close

Opening Product Setup

Ref: O/BAL
Date: 29/11/1999
Quantity: 70.00
Cost Price: 10.00

Save | Cancel

Footer

76 **Sage Line 50 in easy steps**

The In Stock quantity automatically increases when recording an adjustment in a delivery, or posting a credit note for that product. The figure decreases when recording an adjustment out, when a sales order is despatched or when an invoice is posted.

If stock level falls below the re-order level, the item appears red in the Products window and also appears on the Re-order report.

If you do not enter a Cost Price in the Opening Product Setup box, the product cost is recorded as zero. This could affect your finance reports later.

Entering details onto the Product Record

Whilst the Product Record has been designed to accept a considerable amount of detail, not every item is applicable to all products. However, to make reporting more accurate later, you should try and include as much detail as possible about a product when adding records.

Not all of the boxes on the Product Record will accept user entry though. Sage Line 50 calculates or generates the following information and enters it for you. It cannot be directly edited.

Allocated	This figure shows the quantity of the product which has been partly or fully allocated on the sales order, but which has not yet been despatched.
Free Stock	Sage Line 50 calculates the Free Stock as being the In Stock total minus the Allocated stock total.
On Order	Using the Purchase Orders option, this is the quantity of the product which has been put 'on order'.
Last Ord Qty	This shows the amount of stock ordered when the last purchase order for this product was put 'on order'.
Last Ord Date	This shows the date of the last purchase order raised for this product after it had been put on order.
Cost Price	This is the latest cost price for the product item, entered using the Opening Balance option, the Adjustments In option, Purchase Order Processing or the Global Changes option (useful for updating cost prices for all or selected product items).

When running financial or management reports, you must remember that Sage Line 50 will use this latest price even though products already in stock may have actually cost more or less. This may, on occasion, give distorted figures, such as when calculating the total cost value of a product item in stock.

Product Defaults

To save time and make the process of creating new product records easier, Sage Line 50 lets you set up certain product defaults.

Use the Departments option from the Settings menu to quickly set up department names.

Whenever a new product record is created, certain regular details, e.g. Nominal Code, Tax Code, Department etc., are asked for. If you use a recording system where these codes remain the same for most of your products, default settings can be set up which will then appear automatically in each new product record without you having to enter them every time. You set up product defaults as follows:

1 From the Sage Line 50 menu bar, select Settings, then Product Defaults.

2 Enter the Nominal Code to be used by default whenever you create orders and product invoices.

3 Select the VAT rate code from the drop-down list box.

Sage Line 50 stores up to a maximum of six decimal places for rounding up for both product quantity and sales price.

4 Describe the unit of sale here, e.g. 'each', 'box'.

5 Select Category and Department default.

Product Defaults

Details

Defaults

Nominal Code	4000
Tax Code	T1 17.50
Unit of Sale	
Category	1
Department	0

Decimal Precison

Quantity D.P.	0
Unit D.P.	2

OK   Cancel

If you set the Unit DP to a value greater than 2, the net amount on any product invoice you create will still be rounded to 2 decimal places.

6 Enter number of decimal places for quantities.

7 Enter number of decimal places for your product sales prices.

8 Click OK to save or Cancel to abandon any changes.

Using Criteria

Use the Amounts tab to apply criteria to monetary data types, such as Cost Price and Sales Price.

Using criteria speeds up the process of searching for specific product records, for example to show products which match a particular description, or those with a stock level that has fallen below the required re-order level. The following example shows how to set up Criteria to restrict Product Records to only those with less than 50 in stock:

1 From the Products window, click on the Criteria button to bring up the Criteria window.

2 Click on the Amounts tab.

Wildcards, such as * can be used in the Value text boxes.

3 Select the check box of the data type required.

4 Select appropriate Criteria.

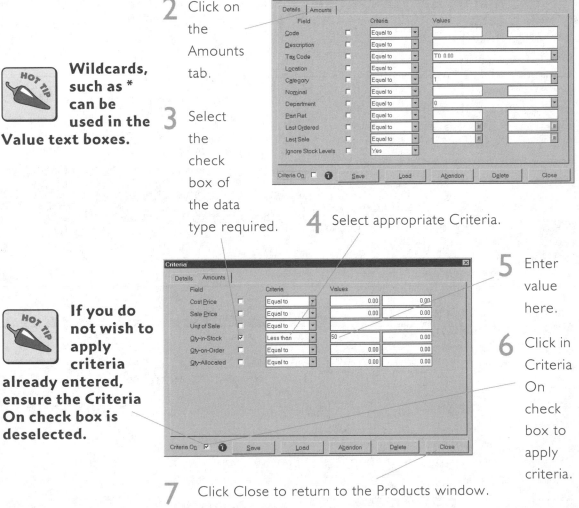

If you do not wish to apply criteria already entered, ensure the Criteria On check box is deselected.

5 Enter value here.

6 Click in Criteria On check box to apply criteria.

7 Click Close to return to the Products window.

Bill of Materials

Use the Transfer button from the Products window to increase the stock levels of your product assemblies.

This term relates to a product you hold in stock made up from other products you keep. The made up product is sometimes known as a product assembly and is said to have a Bill of Materials. For example, a first aid kit is a product assembly consisting of various components – bandages, tablets, plasters, cream etc.

For businesses selling a product made up of other products, it is useful to set up a Bill of Materials. In Sage Line 50 this feature keeps track of stock levels and can automatically calculate how many products you can make up for sale from the stock you hold and at what cost price. To set up a Bill of Materials for a product:

The Bill of Materials table details each individual component for the product assembly on a separate line. Sage Line 50 allows for a maximum of ten components per product assembly.

1 From the Products window, select the product you wish to set up a Bill of Materials for, then click Record.

2 Click the BOM tab from the Product Record.

3 Enter Product Code for each item.

See how many product assemblies you can make up by using the Calculate button and looking in the Available to Makeup box.

Product Code	Asm	Link	Description	Qty
BIN001	0	1	Plain Bin	1.00
BST001	0	1	Binding Strip	2.00
COV001	0	1	Floral Cover	1.00
GLU001	0	1	Adhesive	1.00

Product Record — Details | Memo | BOM | Sales | Graph | Activity | Discount

Product Code: BBB   Description: Waste Bin - Floral   Asm: 1   Lnk: 0

Available to Makeup: 35.00   Calculate

Save   Abandon   Delete   Back   Next   Close

4 Enter quantity required for product assembly.

5 Click Calculate to see how many you can make.

6 Click Save to store Bill of Materials, or Abandon to start again.

Use the Finder button to quickly locate Product Codes.

7 Click Close.

Viewing Transactions

To amend values for all, or a selected group of products within the Product Record, select the Global Changes option from the Tools menu.

Use Copy Matrix button to copy discount structure from another discounted product.

Use a range of 2D and 3D chart types to compare how you did last year with this year's budget.

Sage Line 50 provides you with four different methods of discounting sales to your Customers.

The Sales Tab

You can use this dialog box to view the sales value and quantity sold for your selected product during the financial year on a month by month basis. With a record selected:

1 From the Product Record click on the Sales tab.

2 Use scroll bar to view different months.

Product Record

Details | Memo | BOM | Sales | Graph | Activity | Discount

		Sales Value			Qty Sold		
Month	Sales Cost	Actuals	Budgets	Prior Year	Actuals	Budgets	Prior Year
Jun	0.00	0.00	0.00	0.00	0.00	0.00	0.00
Jul	0.00	0.00	0.00	0.00	0.00	0.00	0.00
Aug	30.00	60.00	0.00	0.00	6.00	0.00	0.00
Sep	20.00	36.00	0.00	0.00	4.00	0.00	0.00
Oct	5.00	10.00	0.00	0.00	1.00	0.00	0.00
Nov	0.00	0.00	0.00	0.00	0.00	0.00	0.00
Dec	0.00	0.00	0.00	0.00	0.00	0.00	0.00
Future	45.00	87.75	0.00	0.00	9.00	0.00	0.00
Totals	135.00	262.75	0.00	0.00	27.00	0.00	0.00

Date Of Last Sale   14/11/1999

Save | Abandon | Delete | Back | Next | Close

3 Click Close.

Product Discounts

1 From the Product Record click on the Discount tab.

2 Enter quantity for customer to qualify for a discount.

Product Record

Details | Memo | BOM | Sales | Graph | Activity | Discount

Discount A | Discount B | Discount C | Discount D | Discount E

Discount	Quantity	Discount %	Value
Level 1	15.00	5.00	9.50
Level 2	20.00	6.00	9.40
Level 3	25.00	6.50	9.35
Level 4	30.00	7.00	9.30
Level 5	35.00	7.50	9.25
Level 6	40.00	8.00	9.20
Level 7	45.00	8.50	9.15
Level 8	0.00	0.00	0.00

Copy Matrix

Save | Abandon | Delete | Back | Next | Close

3 Enter % Discount.

4 Discounted value is calculated for you.

5 Repeat as required.

6 Click Save to store entries, then Close.

Product Activity

To print a report of your product activity, use the Reports option from the Products window and run the activity layout.

This feature allows the user to view product stock movement. Adjustments of goods in and out, stock transfers, current quantities in stock, on order and allocated prove invaluable when trying to fulfil orders or analyse and track the movement of stock.

You can decide when you no longer wish to retain certain transactions on your system by using the Clear Stock option. This facility enables transactions to be cleared from your Product History prior to a specific date.

It is important that you understand the following terms when trying to calculate the availability of stock and to understand the product reports produced by Sage Line 50:

Where activities have been cleared at the month end, they will be shown as carried forward totals with a Ref. of O/BAL, usually at the top of the list.

Tp: A code to identify the type of transaction, where:

     AI   =   Adjustment In.

     AO =   Adjustment Out.

     MI   =   Movement In (product transfer only).

     MO =   Movement Out (product transfers only).

     GR =   Goods Returned (via credit notes).

     GO =   Goods Out (via sales orders and product invoices).

     GI   =   Goods In (via purchase orders)

To clear stock transactions, choose the Period End option from the Tools menu and click the Clear Stock option. Adjustments made are brought forward as opening balances, showing quantities used, in AI and MI.

Used: This is the sum of all the AO (Adjustments Out), GO (Goods Out) and MO (Movements Out) quantities for the product within the specified date range.

Cost: If the transaction line refers to an AI (Adjustment In), GI (Goods In), GR (Goods Returned) or MI (Movement In), this shows the cost price.

Sale: Where a transaction line refers to an AO (Adjustment Out), GO (Goods Out) or GR (Goods Returned), this shows the sales price.

Viewing a product's activity is also available using the Activity tab from the Product Record window.

Qty on Order   This is the product quantity which has been ordered and placed on order using the Purchase Order option, but not yet delivered.

Qty Allocated   This shows the product quantity that has been Allocated to sales orders using the Sales Order Processing option.

Qty in Stock   This is the sum of all the AI (Adjustments In), MI (Movements In), GI (Goods In) and GR (Goods Received), less the quantity used for the specified period.

Unless you change the default date range, all product activity will be displayed.

Qty Available   The Quantity in Stock less Quantity Allocated.

To view Activity from the Products window:

1 Click on the product or products required.

2 Click on Activity to bring up the Date Range box.

3 Enter From and To date.

Use Finder button to select another Product Code if required.

4 Click OK.

Date Range

Date Range

From: 01/01/1980

To: 31/12/2099

OK   Cancel

Use the < and > buttons to move between selected products.

Activity

Transactions

| Product Code | AAA | | Description | Automatic Kettle |
| Cat Number | | | Category Name | |

Tp	Date	Ref.	Details	Qty	Used	Cost	Sale
	01/01/1999		Bfwd Product	9.00			
AI	08/11/1999	O/BAL	Bfwd Product	50.00	35.00	40.00	
GI	08/11/1999	112	Goods In	15.00		40.00	
GO	28/10/1999	1	Goods Out	20.00		40.00	53.98
GO	27/10/1999	2	Goods Out	15.00		40.00	53.98

| Qty on Order | 0.00 | Qty in Stock | 39.00 |
| Qty Allocated | 0.00 | Qty Available | 39.00 |

Range   <   >   Close

5 Click Range to enter new Date Range.

6 Click Close when finished.

Product Adjustments

The In and Out options from the Product window are used to record adjustments to your product's stock levels, such as when stock is received into stores, an order is returned, or stock is taken out as a damaged.

The In button is used to enter any increase in a product's available stock, whilst the Out option is for recording a decrease.

If there is a discrepancy after a stock take, enter additional stock by using the In button.

To make Adjustments In

1 From the Products window click the In option.

2 Enter Product Code.

3 Enter quantity in.

Cost prices are important to the valuation of the stock as product levels are controlled on a first in, first out basis.

4 Enter Date & Ref.

5 Enter Cost.

5 Click Save to store changes and Close.

The Out button is used to record any miscellaneous product movements which decrease a product's available stock level and where no product invoice has been raised

Use the Goods Received Note number as a Reference.

To make Adjustments Out

1 Click the Out option.

2 Enter Product Code.

3 Enter quantity and click Save and Close.

Product Transfers

You can only use a product code which has been previously set up to be a product assembly using the BOM option.

This feature is used for increasing the In Stock quantity of Product Assemblies using components currently in stock. The Product Assemblies are set up using the Bill of Materials option (see page 80).

When using the Product Transfer option the cost price for each Product Assembly is calculated for you by Sage Line 50, by adding together the cost price of each component.

To make a product transfer from the Products window:

1 Click on the Transfer button.

2 Click on the Product Code Finder button.

3 Select Product Assembly Code.

Use the Calendar if you need to make a quick date change.

4 Click OK.

Code	Name
AAA	Automatic Kettle
BBB	Waste Bin - Floral
BIN001	Plain Bin
BST001	Binding Strip
CHOC01	Box of Chocolates - 500 gms
COV001	Floral Cover
GLU001	Adhesive

Criteria   New   OK   Cancel

Stock Transfers

Transfers

Product Code	Details	Date	Ref.	Qty	In stock	On order	Allocated
BBB	Waste Bin - Floral	15/11/1999		10.00	65.00	0.00	0.00

Save   Abandon   Close

If you do not have sufficient stock of components to make up the quantity you have entered, Sage Line 50 will display a warning.

5 Check Details and Date.

6 Enter Quantity required here.

7 Click Save to record entries or Abandon to start again.

8 Click Close.

Product Reports

The Product Reports option allows you to print out a wide range of useful pre-prepared product related reports. These reports show such things as product details and movements, and will help you to keep track of what your company has in stock, its financial value etc.

Additional product reports tailored to your business needs can be created using the Report Designer (See Chapter Twelve). To run a Product Report:

Use the Criteria button on the Products window when you need to select specific ranges of products to report on.

1 From the Products window click Reports to bring up the Product Reports list.

2 Click on the report you require.

3 Ensure Preview is selected.

Use the Product Audit Trail to quickly track the movement of stock.

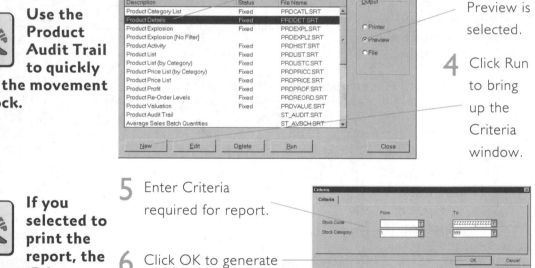

4 Click Run to bring up the Criteria window.

5 Enter Criteria required for report.

6 Click OK to generate report.

If you selected to print the report, the Windows Print dialog box appears. Use this to select which pages to print and change your printer settings if necessary.

7 Click Print, then OK and Close.

Invoices

This chapter shows you how to produce invoices and credit notes for your products and services. Customers, Products and Nominal Accounts are directly linked to Invoicing so the invoices produced automatically update the relevant ledgers. Any raised invoices not posted or printed can be monitored. Quotes and Proformas can also be generated.

Covers

The Invoicing Toolbar | 88

Invoicing | 89

The Product Invoice | 90

Printing an Invoice | 92

The Service Invoice | 93

The Skeleton Invoice | 95

Product Credit Note | 96

Service Credit Note | 97

Updating your Ledgers | 98

Printing for Batch Invoicing | 99

Producing Reports | 100

Chapter Seven

The Invoicing Toolbar

This toolbar provides facilities for generating invoices, quotes, proformas and credit notes for the goods you sell and the services you provide. Ledgers can be automatically updated, transactions printed out and reports generated for analysis purposes.

  To Create or View a Product Invoice.

  To Create or View a Service Invoice.

  To Create or View a Product Credit Note.

  To Create or View a Service Credit Note.

  To Print an Invoice or Credit Note.

  To Update your Ledgers.

  To Run Invoicing Reports.

Invoicing

Sage Line 50 generates invoice numbers in sequence, normally starting at 1. However, you can start with your own numbering system, of up to seven digits. This will be incremented for you each time a new invoice is generated.

Processing manually generated invoices, or batch invoicing, has already been referred to in Chapters Two and Three. Briefly, Chapter Two (Customers) explains how to log invoices and credit notes within the system after they have been produced and sent to customers. Chapter Three (Suppliers) explains how to record invoices and credit notes you receive from your suppliers.

Invoicing deals with Sage Line 50 generated invoices, of which there are two basic types. Firstly there is the Product Invoice, which is used for invoicing customers for the products you sell. Each line of the invoice can be used for recording specific product items. Early discount settlement can be offered on these invoices and carriage charges applied.

As you create invoices they are displayed on the Invoicing list box, one line per invoice. This list also includes any product invoices you created using the Sales Order Processing option.

Meanwhile the Service Invoice is used to invoice customers you have provided a service for. An unlimited amount of text can be entered into the invoice describing the services supplied. Discount settlement can be applied and carriage charges recorded.

Because Sage Line 50 generates these invoices, all the relevant details are automatically recorded and posted for you when you are ready. For invoices where the same information is entered regularly, the Memorise option saves the invoice as a template. This template can then be recalled when required and updated with the new information, saving valuable time.

Also within Invoicing is the facility to generate credit notes for your customers, where products or services for example, have not been received or had to be returned. When these transactions are posted, the ledgers will be updated automatically.

Invoices remain in the Invoicing window list box until removed using the Delete option.

You do, of course, need to keep track of your invoicing. Use the report facility regularly to print out a list of Invoices not yet printed or posted, or to check on stock requirements or shortfalls for the invoices you have generated using this Invoicing option.

The Product Invoice

To retrieve and edit an existing invoice, simply select the invoice from the Invoicing window and click Product.

You cannot amend a product invoice where the quantity was entered using the Sales Order Processing option.

As well as normal product codes, you can also enter special non-product codes:

S1 = Non-product item with price and VAT amount.

S2 = Non-product item, exempt for VAT (Tax code T0).

M = Non-product item with additional message, no price or VAT amount.

To invoice your customers for the products you sell, use the Product option from the Invoicing toolbar (be careful not to confuse this button with the Products icon on the Sage Line 50 toolbar). To create an Invoice click Invoicing on the main toolbar, then do the following:

1 Click Product from the Invoicing toolbar.

2 Enter the tax point date if different from current date.

3 Type Sales Order No. if applicable here.

4 Enter Customer Account Code.

5 Customer details appear here.

6 Enter the Product Code here (use Finder button).

7 Enter Quantity here.

8 Repeat Steps 6 & 7 for further products, then click Save to finish.

9 Click Close.

Any changes made to the delivery details are not saved back to the Customer Record.

Product Invoice Order Details

You can record useful additional Order Details on your Invoice if necessary:

1 Click on Order Details tab.

2 Enter Delivery Address.

3 Enter any Notes if required.

4 Enter Customer Order Details, especially Order No.

Using the Footer Details tab you can enter or amend any settlement terms, and add any analysis conditions that you wish to apply to the entire invoice, e.g. the Tax Code, Nominal Account Code and Department.

Product Invoice Footer Details

Further details, such as Carriage and Settlement Terms, go in the Footer Details:

5 Click on Footer Details tab.

6 Enter any Carriage details here.

7 Record Settlement Terms here.

For a payment which has already been received and can be allocated against a product invoice, record it using the Payment Details tab.

8 Enter any Global detail changes.

9 Click Save.

10 Click Close to finish.

Printing an Invoice

When using the Invoicing option to create invoices and credit notes, you can choose either to print straight away or save them as a batch for printing later using the Print option on the Invoicing Toolbar.

Sage Line 50 gives you the option to print Invoices or Credit Notes either immediately, or at a later date. To print straight away after you have entered all of the details, instead of clicking Save do the following:

1 Click Print.

2 Click on Yes to confirm saving.

3 Select a suitable file layout.

4 Check Output is set to Printer.

5 Click Run.

6 Click OK to print.

7 Select Preview then click OK.

8 Click Close to finish.

Batching invoices or credit notes is useful if you only have one printer. You simply load the correct stationery in the printer once, then print them all in one go.

If no records are selected from the list in the Invoicing window, all non-printed invoices or credit notes will be printed.

The Service Invoice

To avoid having to re-create the same invoice details all the time, store a template using the Memorise button.

To invoice customers for the services you provide instead of products you sell, you should generate a Service Invoice using the Service button from the Invoicing Toolbar. An unlimited amount of text can be entered to describe the services provided, and each service can be analysed to a different nominal account. Settlement discounts can also be applied as well as recording carriage charges.

As with Product Invoices, a Service Invoice can be saved to print in a batch later or printed straight away. At this point you have the option to update the ledgers at the same time or leave them until a more appropriate time.

Sage Line 50 warns you if a selected customer account has been marked as 'on hold' on the Customer Record.

1 Click Service from the Invoicing toolbar.

2 Type correct date if different from current date.

3 Enter Order Number.

4 Enter Customer Code.

Select a service item and click on the Edit box or Press F3 to view item details. If required, you can alter the Posting Details or enter a Job Reference.

If you make a mistake, simply click Abandon and start again.

5 Type service Details here.

6 Enter net Price.

7 Repeat Steps 5 & 6 as required.

8 Click Save to print later, or Print to print now.

9 Click Close to finish.

...cont'd

Any changes made to the delivery details are not saved back to the Customer Record.

Using the Footer Details tab you can enter or amend any settlement terms you operate with your customer. You can also add any analysis conditions that you wish to apply to the entire invoice.

For payments you have received which can be allocated against the invoice, record the details using the Payment Details tab.

Service Invoice Order Details

You can record useful additional Order Details on your Service Invoice if required:

1   Click on Order Details tab.

2   Enter Delivery Address.

3   Enter any Notes if required.

4   Enter Customer Order Details, such as Order No.

Service Invoice Footer Details

You can record details such as Carriage and Settlement Terms in the Footer Details box:

5   Click on Footer Details tab.

6   Enter any Carriage details here.

7   Record Settlement Terms here.

8   Enter any Global detail changes.

9   Click Save.

10   Click Close to finish.

The Skeleton Invoice

For information that is regularly repeated when creating an invoice, use the Memorise option to store the invoice as a template. You can then recall this template as and when required, and update it with the new information, thus saving valuable time and reduce keying errors.

This facility is available for both Product and Service Invoices, as well as the Product and Service Credit Notes.

Any unwanted skeleton invoices can be deleted using the Edit menu (recall option).

| In the Details box enter regularly used details only, such as Customer A/C Ref. and item Details. Omit the Price.

When you load your skeleton, all the details that you saved appear automatically.

```
Service Invoice                                          _ □ ✕

  Details   Order Details   Footer Details   Payment Details

  I.T. Solutions                          Type        Invoice
  Millennium House
  21 Century Road                         Invoice No.  9
  Downtown                                Invoice Date 05/12/1999
  Penns. USA
                                          Order No.
                                          A/C Ref     ITS001

  Details                      Price    Net     VAT
  Training Course Full Day      0.00    0.00    0.00
  Refreshments                  0.00    0.00    0.00
                                        Totals   0.00    0.00
  Item 1 of 2           ✏        Carriage 0.00    0.00
                                        Gross    0.00    0.00

  Save     Abandon    Print    Memorise    Recall    Close
```

A quick way to alter the date in a Date box is to use the up or down cursor keys to move through the days. Pressing Page Up or Page Down moves through the months.

2 Click Memorise.

3 Enter Filename and Description.

4 Click Save.

```
Memorise                                 ✕
  Details

  Filename     [              ]

  Description  [              ]

          Save      Cancel
```

5 When you need to use a layout, click Recall.

6 Select your layout from the list.

7 Click Load.

Product Credit Note

From time to time goods sent to customers may be returned as faulty, past an expiry date etc., or the customer may simply have been overcharged by mistake.

 A VAT only credit note can be raised where a customer has been invoiced and charged tax for goods which are exempt from VAT.

Instead of correcting the original invoice, a Product Credit Note can be issued to the Customer, detailing the amount owing to them. When your ledgers are updated, the necessary postings will be made to reflect this amendment. Do the following to create a Product Credit Note:

1 Click Credit from the Invoicing toolbar.

2 Enter date for the credit note if different from current date.

3 Type your Order No. if applicable here.

4 Enter Customer Account Code.

 The first time you create a credit note Sage Line 50 starts the numbering from 1 but you can use your own number system if you wish (up to 7 digits).

Product Credit Note

Details | Order Details | Footer Details

Business Exhibitions
44 Which Way
Showtown
SH0 5TN

Credit No. 134
Credit Date 15/11/1999
Order No.
A/C Ref BUS001

Product Code	Description	Qty	Net	V.A.T.
APBU	Cancel - see tran 2345	1.00	9.75	1.71

Item 1 of 1

Totals	9.75	1.71
Carriage	0.00	0.00
Gross	0.00	11.46

Save | Abandon | Print | Memorise | Recall | Close

 One-off details can be entered against each Credit Note product item to record, for example, changes to customer discounts, address, unit price or simply to add a short comment.

5 Customer details appear here.

6 Enter the Product Code.

7 Enter Quantity here.

8 Repeat Steps 6 & 7 as required, then click Save to finish.

9 Click Close.

Service Credit Note

 If you have a standard type of Credit Note that you use regularly, create a template for it and save it using the Memorise button. You can then recall this template as and when necessary.

A Service Credit Note can be used where, for example, customers have been charged or overcharged for a service they have not received. In this case you would issue a Service Credit Note detailing the changes made and the amount owing to the customer. When the ledgers are updated, the necessary postings will be made.

This method replaces editing the original service invoice and regenerating a new one:

1 Click SrvCredit from the Invoicing toolbar.

2 Type correct date if different from current date.

3 Enter Order Number.

4 Enter Customer Code.

 To edit an existing credit note, enter the credit note number in the Credit No. box and press TAB.

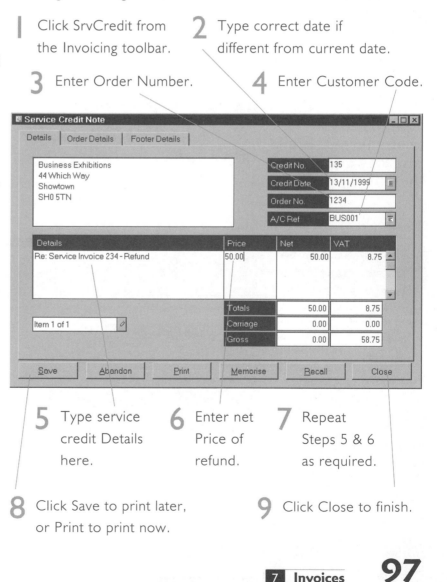

Choosing the Save button saves the credit note for printing later in a 'batch'. To print the credit note straight away and update the ledgers, choose the Print button instead.

5 Type service credit Details here.

6 Enter net Price of refund.

7 Repeat Steps 5 & 6 as required.

8 Click Save to print later, or Print to print now.

9 Click Close to finish.

Updating your Ledgers

By regularly updating your stock records, you may find you now have enough free stock to complete outstanding sales orders.

After Updating, you can view the changes to the customer ledger and stock by using the Activity option.

Use the Clear button to deselect all before starting.

Always make sure you select at least one Invoice or Credit Note before using the Update function otherwise Sage Line 50 will ask you if you want to process ALL non-posted invoices and credit notes.

After creating your invoices and credit notes, the Update function is used to transfer details to the customer and nominal ledgers and, if appropriate, to amend product records.

Sage Line 50 gives you the option to print the update report immediately, preview it first so that you can select only certain pages for printing, or to save the report as a file. To perform an Update, do the following:

1 From the Invoicing window select the invoices and credit notes for updating.

2 Click Update to display the Output options.

Invoicing

No.	Type	Date	Name	Amount	Printed	Posted
1	Inv	28/10/1999	Palmer Energy Ltd	1268.53	Yes	Yes
2	Inv	27/10/1999	I.T. Solutions	951.40	Yes	Yes
4	Inv	10/11/1999	I.T. Solutions	413.31	Yes	Yes
5	Inv	15/11/1999	Palmer Energy Ltd	551.08	Yes	Yes
6	Inv	05/12/1999	I.T. Solutions	5.17	Yes	Yes
7	Inv	05/12/1999	I.T. Solutions	126.85	Yes	Yes
8	Inv	05/12/1999	Palmer Energy Ltd	275.54	Yes	Yes
9	Inv	06/12/1999	Palmer Energy Ltd	47.00	Yes	

Criteria | Swap | Clear | Delete | Close

Update Ledgers

Output
- Printer
- Preview
- File

OK | Cancel

3 In the Output box click Preview.

4 Click OK to generate the update.

5 On the report, click Print to bring up the Windows Print dialog box, then click OK to print.

6 Click Close to return to the Invoicing window, then Close again.

98

Printing for Batch Invoicing

You can reprint your invoices as many times as you wish.

When you created Invoices or Credit Notes, both Product or Service, you may have decided to leave printing them until later as a batch. This can often save time when setting up file layouts and having to change the printer stationery.

For example, you may have created two Service invoices which now need printing. You would do the following:

Use the Criteria button if you wish to print a number of invoices or credit notes that match a particular condition.

I From the Invoicing window, select the invoices and credit notes for printing.

2 Click on the Print icon.

Select the correct layout file for printing your invoice or credit notes, depending upon which type of printer and paper size you are using.

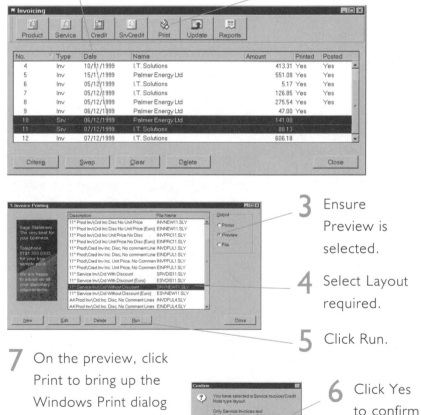

3 Ensure Preview is selected.

4 Select Layout required.

5 Click Run.

Standard layouts can be edited or new layouts created where necessary.

7 On the preview, click Print to bring up the Windows Print dialog box, then click OK to print.

6 Click Yes to confirm layout.

8 Click Close to return to the Invoicing window.

Producing Reports

The Reports option allows you to produce a wide range of reports about your product and service invoices, as well as your credit notes. Use these reports regularly to keep your business up to date. To print an invoice report:

Save time: instead of searching through all your invoices for those not yet posted, use the Invoices Not Posted report.

1 Click Reports from the Invoicing toolbar.

2 Select report required.

3 Ensure Preview is selected.

4 Click Run to generate report.

Use the Invoices Not Printed report regularly to keep up to date with sending out Invoices.

Alternatively, use the Criteria button on the Invoicing window to only list invoices not yet printed, posted, product only or service only etc.

5 Check report then click Print.

6 Click OK to print report.

7 Click Close to finish.

Processing Sales Orders

This chapter shows you how to keep track of your Sales Orders. You will learn how to allocate and despatch stock to these orders to keep your stock levels up-to-date. You will be shown how to automatically generate a Sales Invoice for each despatch you make and how to print Sales Orders, Delivery Notes and a variety of reports.

Covers

The Sales Order Processing Toolbar | 102

The Sales Order | 103

Allocating Stock | 105

Despatching Sales Orders | 106

Amending & Printing Sales Orders | 107

Sales Orders Reports | 108

Chapter Eight

The Sales Order Processing Toolbar

The SOP toolbar provides a number of features for creating a sales order and then controlling the allocation of stock to that order. Once you are ready to deliver the stock, you can despatch it and Sage Line 50 will automatically handle the stock record updates. From this toolbar you can also print sales orders, whilst information regarding sales order processing can be easily obtained by using the various report layouts already provided for you.

 To Create or View a Sales Order.

 To Allocate Stock to a Sales Order.

 To Despatch a Sales Order.

 To Make Changes to a Sales Order.

 To Print a Sales Order.

 To Run Sales Order Reports.

The Sales Order

On a Network, if a number of users create Sales Orders at the same time and one order is abandoned, the order numbers will no longer run consecutively because the abandoned number will not be used.

Sales orders can be created for the products you supply and sent to customers by using the Enter option from the Sales Order Processing toolbar. Details from your Product records are automatically entered onto the Sales Orders whilst extra details can also be added, such as a delivery address, a customer order number for future reference or a settlement discount etc.

To create a Sales Order, click SOP from the Sage Line 50 toolbar, then do the following:

1 Click Enter from the Sales Order Processing toolbar.

2 Type required date if different to current date.

4 Customer details appear here.

3 Enter Customer Account Code.

Use the Message box (i.e., the product code M) to add any text to the main body of the sales order, for example, 'goods supplied free'.

To include special one-off details against a sales item, click the Edit button from the Description box.

5 Enter the Product Code here (use Finder button).

6 Enter Quantity ordered here.

7 Repeat Steps 5 & 6 for additional products, then if finished click Save.

8 Click Close.

...cont'd

Each line of the Sales Order is treated separately for product discount purposes. Make sure you only enter each product code once if a customer qualifies for a product discount.

Once a Sales Order has been despatched in part or full, you cannot decrease the quantity of any product ordered to less than the quantity despatched.

Sage Line 50 will generate an invoice and enter the Invoice Number for you automatically when the order is Despatched.

Sales Order Details

On the previous page you were shown how to create a Sales Order and save it immediately if no further details needed entering. Sage Line 50, however, gives you the option to enter additional details about the order, such as where it should be delivered if different from the main address etc.

From the Sales Order window, do the following to enter additional order details:

1 Click on the Order Details tab.

2 Enter Delivery Address here if required.

3 Record any Notes here.

```
┌─ Sales Order ─────────────────────────────── _ □ X ┐
│  Details   Order Details   Footer Details            │
│  ┌─ Delivery Address ──────┐   ┌─ Notes ──────────┐  │
│  │                         │   │                  │  │
│  │                         │   │                  │  │
│  │                         │   │                  │  │
│  │                         │   │                  │  │
│  └─────────────────────────┘   └──────────────────┘  │
│  ┌─ Customer Order Details ─┐   ┌─ Order Status ───┐  │
│  │ Customer Order No. [    ]│   │ Invoice No. [   ] │  │
│  │ Customer Tel. No.  [    ]│   │ Allocation  [   ] │  │
│  │ Customer Contact   [    ]│   │ Despatch    [   ] │  │
│  │ Order Taken By     [    ]│   │ Due Despatch [  ▾]│  │
│  └──────────────────────────┘   └──────────────────┘  │
│  [Save] [Abandon] [Print] [Complete] [Memorise] [Recall] [Close] │
└──────────────────────────────────────────────────────┘
```

4 Enter any relevant Customer Order Details, such as a Customer Order Number.

5 You may wish to enter Due Despatch date here.

6 Click Save when finished.

7 Click Close.

Allocating Stock

Use the Criteria feature to filter out orders and display only the ones you wish to work with.

If Sage Line 50 cannot allocate all of the necessary stock to the order, a message box is displayed giving suggestions and possible reasons why not.

To view Sales Order details simply double-click on the item.

If there is insufficient stock for a Sales Order, the Status 'Part' appears in the Sales Order Processing window. Fully allocated orders display 'Full'.

Once a Sales Order has been created, stock needs allocating to it before any despatches can be recorded for the Order. Using the Allocate option from the Sales Order Processing toolbar automatically allocates the necessary stock needed for the selected Sales Order.

Sometimes there is insufficient stock available to complete an Order, in which case the Order will be marked as 'Part' complete. There may be times when you have enough stock, but wish to only send part of the Order. In this case you would use the Amend option to make changes to the Order. To allocate batched Sales Orders, do the following from within the Sales Order Processing window:

2 Click Allocate.

1 Click on the Sales Orders you wish to Allocate.

3 Click Yes to Confirm Allocation of stock.

4 Note change in Sales Order Status.

5 Click Close.

Despatching Sales Orders

To Despatch a batch of Sales Orders, select the required Sales Orders by clicking on them to highlight, or use the Swap and Clear buttons.

Once stock is allocated to your sales orders, it can be despatched at any time. The Despatch option also updates the product records and creates a Product Invoice for the order, as well as printing a Delivery Note.

The product invoices created through Sales Order Processing appears in the Invoicing window. These invoices can be edited, but you cannot change the quantity of the product despatched. They can then be printed and posted to the sales and nominal ledgers in the same manner as invoices created using the Invoicing option.

If only part of an order is despatched, Sage Line 50 creates an invoice for that part. This means that when the order is fully despatched, there will be more than one invoice for it.

I From the Sales Order Processing window, select the required Sales Orders.

2 Click Despatch.

3 Click Yes to print Delivery Notes if required.

4 Select Delivery Note layout.

5 Click Run.

Click the Complete button from the Sales Order window to automatically save the order, Allocate stock to it and record the Despatch all in one go.

6 Click Yes to confirm creation of invoices and update of stock.

7 Print required Delivery Notes, then Close all windows.

Amending & Printing Sales Orders

When you Amend the allocation of stock to a sales order, the allocated status of the order in the Sales Orders window may change to either Full, Part or no status at all.

If you have allocated stock to a sales order, but have not yet despatched all of it, you can amend this allocation. This allows you to despatch a full order by reducing the stock allocation of another customer's order, hence perhaps reducing the number of customers waiting.

To amend the allocation of stock on a sales order

1 Select the Order from the Sales Order Processing window and click Amend.

2 Amend the Allocation.

By batching your orders, you can print them all out together after setting up the printer with the correct sales order stationery.

3 Click Close and note any change in Status.

Printing Batched Orders

1 Select orders for printing from Sales Order Processing window and Click Print

Always Preview anything to be printed out to save wasting paper.

2 Select layout required.

3 Click Run.

4 Click Print, then Close.

Sales Orders Reports

Sage Line 50 provides you with a large variety of reports to help you run the Sales Order side of your business. For example, you have the facility to print a picking list for your warehouse from a particular order or the sales order shortage report to show you shortfalls in the stock.

These reports are generated from the information entered when you created a sales order. To generate, for example, a Sales Order Picking List:

 Regularly use the Sales Orders to be Invoiced report to keep up to date with your invoicing.

1 From the Sales Order Processing window, click Reports.

2 Select required Layout.

 The number of sales orders included in your reports can be restricted by using the Criteria button on the Sales Orders window.

3 Check Output is set to Preview.

4 Click Run to view report.

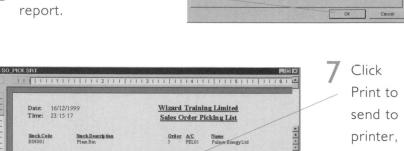

5 Enter Criteria i.e. Sales Order number.

6 Click OK to generate report.

 To check how many despatched orders have gone out for a particular time period, use the Despatched Sales Orders report and apply the Order Date Criteria.

7 Click Print to send to printer, then OK & Close.

Purchase Orders

In this chapter you will learn how to create and print Purchase Orders to send to your suppliers. You will be shown how to monitor orders raised and record deliveries received as well as produce reports to help you keep track of your Purchase Orders.

Covers

Purchase Order Processing Toolbar | 110

Creating a Purchase Order | 111

Placing Purchase Orders 'on order' | 113

Recording Deliveries | 114

Processing Purchases Manually | 115

Recording Deliveries Manually | 116

Printing Batched Purchase Orders | 117

Purchase Order Reports | 118

Chapter Nine

Purchase Order Processing Toolbar

From the POP toolbar you can create and print Purchase Orders as well as make amendments to orders you have already created. You have facilities for recording deliveries and producing useful reports about your Purchase Orders, such as which have been delivered in part or full, or which are still outstanding.

 To Create or View a Purchase Order.

 To Put a Purchase Order 'on order'.

 To Record Purchase Order Deliveries.

 To Make Changes to a Purchase Order.

 To Print a Purchase Order.

 To Run Purchase Order Reports.

Creating a Purchase Order

To edit an existing order simply double-click on it in the Purchase Order Processing window.

You can increase, but not decrease, the quantity for any Purchase Order you have already despatched in full or part.

On a network, if two users create a Purchase Order at the same time and one of the orders is abandoned, the abandoned number will not be re-used, so numbers will not run consecutively.

Use the product code M for non-payment products.

To record order details of any products you buy from a supplier, use the Enter option from the Purchase Order toolbar. Details entered straight onto the Purchase Order screen are taken directly from the product records for you by Sage Line 50.

You can also include additional details, such as delivery address or any settlement discount given to you by your supplier, to the order. To create a Purchase Order click POP from the Sage Line 50 toolbar then follow these steps:

1 Click Enter from the Purchase Orders Processing toolbar.

2 Check required date is entered here.

4 Supplier details appear here.

3 Enter Supplier Account Code.

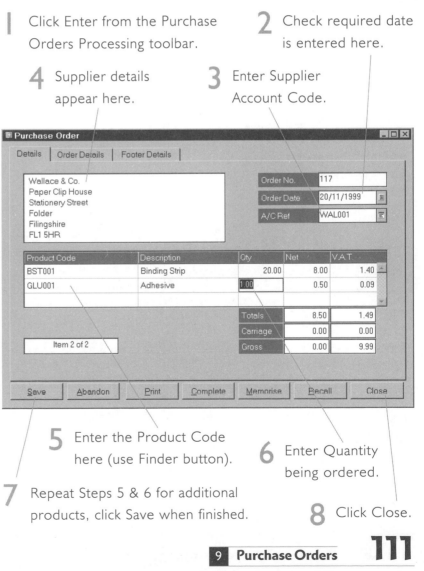

5 Enter the Product Code here (use Finder button).

6 Enter Quantity being ordered.

7 Repeat Steps 5 & 6 for additional products, click Save when finished.

8 Click Close.

...cont'd

If you enter an Account Code that is not already set up, Sage Line 50 automatically invokes the Finder so you can choose another account or create a new one using the New button.

Save your Purchase Order as a Skeleton if you use these details regularly.

If you have already received the products for this Purchase Order, choose the Complete button.

Use the Footer Details tab to record any Carriage or Settlement terms.

Entering Purchase Order Details

You may need to record further details on your Purchase Order, such as delivery details, carriage costs, settlement terms, supplier contact or the name of the person who took your order.

Sage Line 50 lets you do this through the Order Details or Footer Details tabs. From the Purchase Order window, do the following to enter additional order details:

1 Click on the Order Details tab.

2 Enter Delivery Address here if required.

3 Record any Notes you wish to add here.

4 Enter any relevant Supplier Order Details, such as an Order or Telephone Number.

5 You can enter when Delivery is due here.

6 Click Save when all details have been entered.

7 Click Close.

Placing Purchase Orders 'on order'

Once a Purchase Order has been created, it has to be placed 'on order' before any deliveries can be recorded for it. Sage Line 50 then updates each product record with the new order details accordingly.

Use the Order option to automatically place a single or batch of Purchase Orders 'on order', as follows:

 Click the Criteria button to set up a filter to list only the orders you wish to work with.

 To avoid costly mistakes, always check that the status of an order shows ON-ORDER after going through the process of placing it on order.

 To remove a Purchase Order simply highlight it and click on the Delete button.

 You can also put Purchase Orders 'on order' from within the Amend Deliveries option.

1 From the Purchase Order Processing window, highlight all the orders you wish to place 'on order' by clicking on them.

2 Click Order.

3 Click Yes to Confirm you wish to place the selected items 'on order'.

4 Click No here to print a copy of the Purchase Order later, else Yes to print now.

5 Note that items are now ON-ORDER.

6 Click Close.

Recording Deliveries

You can only record deliveries for orders which you have already put 'on order'.

Sage Line 50 automatically makes adjustments for each product that you mark as delivered.

When delivery is recorded for selected Purchase Orders, the Delivered status shows Complete.

When you use the Delivery option it is assumed that you have taken full delivery of all items on the Purchase Order. The Delivery record cannot be altered later.

To automatically record the complete delivery of stock for Purchase Orders use the Deliver option from the Purchase Order Processing toolbar.

You should remember that Sage Line 50 always assumes that you have taken full delivery of all the products needed to complete the selected Purchase Order. If a part delivery needs recording, you must record the delivery using the Amend function (see page 116).

To record Purchase Order deliveries do the following:

1 From the Purchase Order Processing window select any orders you wish to mark as Delivered.

2 Click Deliver.

Purchase Order Processing

	Enter	Order	Deliver	Amend	Print	Reports

No.	Date	Name	Amount	On-Order	Delivered
112	08/11/1999	Wallace & Co.	793.13		COMPLETE
113	22/10/1999	Wallace & Co.	94.00		COMPLETE
114	24/10/1999	Hightown Leisure	88.13		COMPLETE
115	29/10/1999	Wallace & Co.	176.25		COMPLETE
116	18/11/1999	Wallace & Co.	329.00		COMPLETE
117	20/11/1999	Wallace & Co.	9.99	ON-ORDER	
118	22/11/1999	Wallace & Co.	29.38	ON-ORDER	
119	22/11/1999	Hightown Leisure	41.13	ON-ORDER	

Criteria	Swap -	Clear	Delete		Close

Confirm

? Complete deliveries and update stock for selected order(s) ?

Yes   No

3 Click Yes in this box to Confirm delivery and update stock records.

4 Note the Purchase Order now displays as COMPLETE.

5 If finished, Click Close.

Processing Purchases Manually

To check and keep track of your Purchase Orders use the Amend option. In this window you can manually place them 'on order' (thus updating On Order levels for appropriate product records), record full or part deliveries of stock against each order and cancel orders.

 Use the < and > buttons to move between selected Purchase Orders.

Placing a Purchase Order 'on order' manually

You have already learned how to place Purchase Orders 'on order' using the Order button (Page 113). However, Sage Line 50 also allows you to do this manually as follows:

1 From Purchase Order Processing window, select the purchase order you require.

2 Click Amend to bring up the Amend Deliveries window.

 You can cancel a Purchase Order which is 'on order' with the Amend option. Just click Off Order to mark it as cancelled or click Order to put it back 'on order'.

3 Click on the Order button to place 'on order'.

 Cancelling an order does not affect any part deliveries which may have been previously recorded for that Purchase Order.

4 Note the order now looks normal and the full order quantity appears in This Delivery.

5 Click Close.

Recording Deliveries Manually

You use the Deliver button from the Purchase Order Processing toolbar only when you have received full delivery of an order.

If you wish to record part deliveries, then you must use the Amend option, though you can still record full deliveries this way as well, should you need to. To record a Purchase Order part delivery, follow these steps:

 If the order is not 'on order' or has been cancelled, Sage Line 50 will remind you to place the Purchase Order 'on order' to enable you to record the delivery.

1 From the Purchase Order Processing window select the order you wish to record a delivery for.

2 Click Amend.

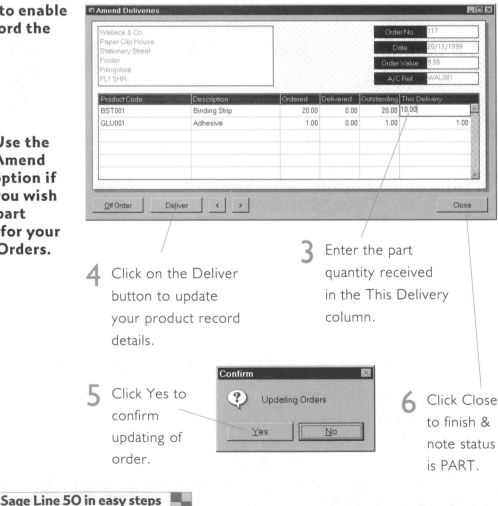

Use the Amend option if you wish to record part deliveries for your Purchase Orders.

3 Enter the part quantity received in the This Delivery column.

4 Click on the Deliver button to update your product record details.

5 Click Yes to confirm updating of order.

6 Click Close to finish & note status is PART.

Printing Batched Purchase Orders

Always make sure you have the correct stationery in the printer as the layout and content of the Purchase Order depends upon the stationery layout file selected.

Rather than print your Purchase Orders straight away you may have chosen to save them until later. This is useful if you only have one printer and need to change the stationery. When you are ready you can then print the orders out in batches.

As with all the printing facilities in Sage Line 50, you can send the Purchase Order direct to the printer, save it as a file or preview it on the screen first. To preview on order and then print it do the following:.

1 From the Purchase Order Processing window, select the order for printing.

2 Click Print.

No.	Date	Name	Amount	On-Order	Delivered
112	08/11/1999	Wallace & Co.	793.13		COMPLETE
113	22/10/1999	Wallace & Co.	94.00		COMPLETE
114	24/10/1999	Hightown Leisure	88.13		COMPLETE
115	29/10/1999	Wallace & Co.	176.25		COMPLETE
116	18/11/1999	Wallace & Co.	329.00		COMPLETE
117	20/11/1999	Wallace & Co.	9.99	ON-ORDER	PART
118	22/11/1999	Wallace & Co.	29.38		COMPLETE
119	22/11/1999	Hightown Leisure	41.13	ON-ORDER	
120	23/11/1999	Wallace & Co.	29.38	ON-ORDER	

To print a specific selection of Purchase Orders use the Criteria button.

Your Purchase Orders can be reprinted as often as you wish.

Description	File Name
11" Purchase Order Inc Line VAT 8 Point	PURVAT11.SLY
11" Purchase Order No Line VAT 10 Point	PURNEW11.SLY
A4 Purchase Order - Inc Line V.A.T. 8 Point	PURVATA4.SLY
A4 Purchase Order - No Line V.A.T. 10 Point	PURNEWA4.SLY

Sage Stationery. The very best for your business.

Telephone: 0191 253 0303 for your free sample pack.

We are happy to advise on all your stationery requirements.

3 Select correct layout.

4 Ensure Preview is checked.

5 Click Run.

6 On the preview, click Print to bring up the Print dialog box, then click OK.

7 Click Close.

Purchase Order Reports

Use the Purchase Order Not Delivered or Part Delivered report to track and monitor your supplies.

Standard reports have already been set up for you to display any outstanding Purchase Orders, or orders which have already been delivered or part delivered. These reports can be previewed on screen, sent to your printer or saved to a file for previewing or printing later.

To generate a report of Purchase Orders not yet delivered, do the following:

1 From the Purchase Order Processing toolbar, click Reports.

2 Select required layout.

3 Check Output is set to Preview.

4 Click Run to view report.

To quickly view details of your Purchase Orders use the Purchase Orders List report.

5 Enter Criteria, if any applies.

6 Click OK to generate the report.

Use the Outstanding Purchase Orders report regularly to keep track of which orders are still outstanding for delivery.

7 Click Print to send to printer, then OK & Close.

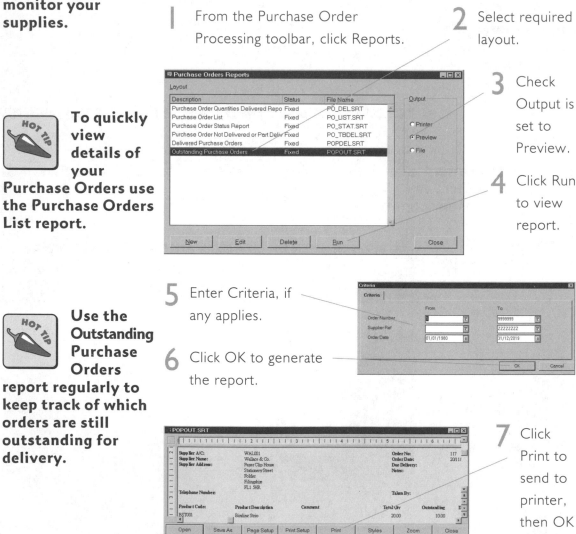

Financials

This Chapter shows you how to generate a variety of Financial reports so you can analyse your business transactions. This includes the Trial Balance, Profit & Loss, the Balance Sheet, the Budget and Prior Year reports. You will learn how to produce an automated VAT Return as well as a detailed Audit Trail, which lists every transaction recorded within the system.

Covers

The Financials Toolbar | 120

The Audit Trail | 121

The Trial Balance | 123

Profit and Loss Report | 124

The Balance Sheet | 125

Quick Ratio Report | 126

The Budget Report | 127

The Prior Year Report | 128

The VAT Return | 129

Financial Reports | 132

Chapter Ten

The Financials Toolbar

From this toolbar you can generate all the financial reports you need to not only keep track of how your business is doing financially but also trace back and find out when certain transactions took place. The Audit Trail is particularly useful as it is a complete record of your transaction activities, whilst the VAT function gives you all the features you need to produce accurate VAT Returns.

 To Produce the Audit Trail.

 Run the Trial Balance Report.

 To Produce the Profit and Loss Report.

 To Produce the Balance Sheet Report.

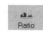 Run the Quick Ratio Report.

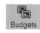 To Produce the Budget Report.

 Run the Prior Year Report.

 To Produce a VAT Return.

 To Run Financial Reports.

The Audit Trail

Deleted transactions always appear in red.

Transaction codes used in the Audit Trail are explained on Page 49.

Sage Line 50 is capable of storing approximately 2,000,000,000 transactions in the Audit Trail (provided your computer has sufficient memory and disk space), so there may be no need to clear it.

When you clear transactions from the Audit Trail, Sage Line 50 brings them forward as opening balances in your financial reports.

The Audit Trail records details about transactions entered into the system and is a very useful source of information for checking and cross reference purposes. It may also be referred to when auditing your accounts.

Sage Line 50 gives you a range of Audit Trail formats providing brief, summary or fully detailed reports which can be previewed, printed directly or saved as a file for use later. A report of deleted transactions can also be printed. Use the Audit Trail regularly to ensure your transactions are being recorded accurately. To view the Audit Trail:

1 From the Sage Line 50 toolbar, click Financials to bring up the Financials window displaying the Audit Trail.

No		Tp	Account	Nominal	Dep	Details	Date	Ref	Ex.Ref
	27	PP	WAL001	1200	0	Purchase Payment	15/10/1999		
	28	JC		1220	0	Bank Transfer	25/10/1999	TRANS	
	29	JD		1200	0	Bank Transfer	25/10/1999	TRANS	
	30	PP	WAL001	1200	0	Purchase Payment	29/10/1999		
	31	JC		1200	0	Bank Transfer	30/10/1999	TRANS	
	32	JD		1240	0	Bank Transfer	30/10/1999	TRANS	
	33	SI	ITS001	4000	0	Automatic Kettle	05/12/1999	7	
	34	SI	PEL01	4000	0	Waste Bin - Floral	05/12/1999	8	
	35	SI	ITS001	4000	0	Adhesive	05/12/1999	6	

Audit | Trial | P and L | Balance | Ratio | Budgets | Prior Yr | VAT | Reports

Close

2 Use both horizontal and vertical arrow buttons and scroll bars to examine all transaction details.

3 When you have finished examining the Audit Trail, click Close.

To print the Audit Trail report

The Criteria box options vary according to the type of Audit Trail report selected.

All reports other than Brief will print in Landscape by default.

You can choose to exclude deleted transactions from your reports and instead, print them as a separate report later.

Print your Audit Trail reports at least every month for reference purposes.

1 From the Financials toolbar click Audit.

2 Select Audit Trail Type required, i.e. Brief.

3 Check Output is set to Preview.

4 Click Run to continue.

5 Enter required Criteria.

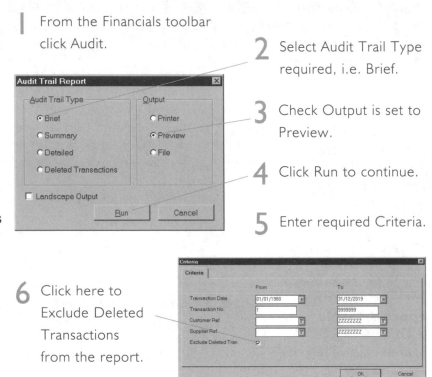

6 Click here to Exclude Deleted Transactions from the report.

7 Click OK to continue.

8 If you want to print the report, click Print, then OK.

9 Close the window.

122 Sage Line 50 in easy steps

The Trial Balance

This report displays a simple listing of current balances in all your nominal ledger accounts. It shows total values for both the debit and credit entries for all the nominal codes containing a balance value.

Because Sage Line 50 controls the double-entry accounting for you, the debit and credit columns will always balance. To produce the Trial Balance report do the following:

You can run this report for any month. It proves a valuable source for management information.

Use the Zoom feature to help you preview the report more accurately before printing.

When you open the Financials window, the display automatically jumps down to the bottom of the list so the most recently entered transactions are displayed.

I From the Financials toolbar click Trial. This brings up the Criteria box.

2 Ensure Preview is selected.

3 Click here and select period required. Scroll down if necessary.

4 Click OK to generate the Trial Balance.

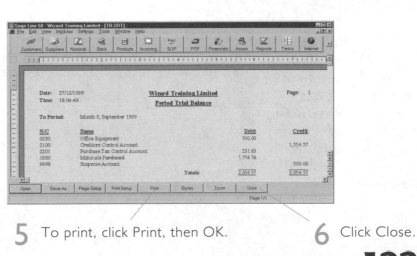

5 To print, click Print, then OK.

6 Click Close.

Profit and Loss Report

Balances are posted before the start of the financial year and so will appear as a prior year adjustment on the balance sheet, not on the Profit and Loss Report.

Unless you have set up your own layout, ensure you choose the Default Layout of Accounts in Step 3, otherwise you will not generate the correct report.

You can set up your own Profit & Loss report layouts using the Chart of Accounts option from the Nominal Ledger toolbar.

This important financial report details whether your business is trading at a profit over a particular period of time. The report can be produced for the current month or a range of consecutive months within your current financial year.

The balances of each of your income and expenditure nominal ledger accounts appear on the standard Profit and Loss report. These categories, i.e. Sales, Purchases, Direct Expenses and Overheads are grouped together and display a sub-total. The Gross Profit/(Loss) and Net Profit/(Loss) amount is also shown.

1 From the Financials window click P and L to bring up the Criteria box.

2 Enter the From and To Period required.

3 Select Default Layout of Accounts (1).

4 Ensure Preview is selected.

5 Click OK to generate P & L report.

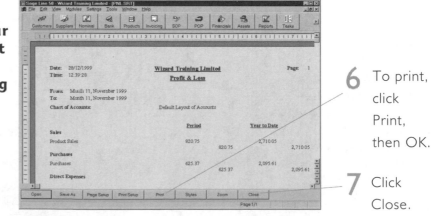

6 To print, click Print, then OK.

7 Click Close.

The Balance Sheet

Use the Balance Sheet regularly to give a summary of your current financial position.

The Balance Sheet details the financial position of a business at a particular moment in time by outlining its assets (what the business owns) and its liabilities (what the business owes). There are two main types of assets, fixed and current. Fixed assets are long-term and have material substance and include, for example, premises, equipment and vehicles, whilst current assets are continually changing and include stock, debtors, cash accounts etc.

The Balance Sheet shows the fixed and current assets, as well as the liabilities. By adding together the assets and subtracting the liabilities, the Balance Sheet shows the Capital, or net assets.

The difference between assets and liabilities is referred to as the company's net assets (or net worth).

1 Click Balance from the Financials toolbar to display the Criteria box.

2 Enter the From and To Period required.

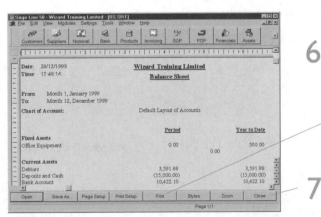

3 Select Default Layout of Accounts (1).

Liabilities consist of both current and long-term. Current liabilities are amounts owing at the balance sheet date and due for repayment within 12 months or less, e.g. trade creditors. Long-term liabilities are amounts due for repayment in more than 12 months, e.g. bank loan.

4 Ensure Preview is selected.

5 Click OK to generate Balance Sheet.

6 To print the Balance Sheet, click Print, then OK.

7 Click Close.

Quick Ratio Report

Using the data available within the system, the Quick Ratio Report allows you to see the current liquidity position of the business. This type of information is necessary for making financial decisions about future investments or developments and will be required by a number of different parties, for example, management, bank managers, shareholders etc.

Use the Quick Ratio Report to see the immediate financial position of your company. This is useful when you are considering future investments etc.

These Ratio Reports highlight both the strengths and the weaknesses in the financial position of your business. Credit and debit balances are compared to show the net balance using previously set up nominal account codes. You can edit the report to include other nominal accounts you wish to compare.

To view or edit the quick ratio report

1 From the Financials window, click Ratio.

2 To edit the nominal accounts, use Finder button to select Nominal Code required.

By editing the Quick Ratio Report you can include different nominal accounts for comparison purposes.

Quick Ratio			
N/C Ref	N/C Name	Debit	Credit
1100	Debtors Control Account	3591.88	0.00
1103	Prepayments	0.00	0.00
1200	Bank Current Account	10422.10	0.00
1210	Bank Deposit Account	0.00	0.00
1220	Building Society Account	0.00	15000.00
1230	Petty Cash	0.00	0.00
1240	Company Credit Card	2000.00	0.00
1250	Credit Card Receipts	0.00	0.00
2100	Creditors Control Account	0.00	506.17
2109	Accruals	0.00	0.00
2200	Sales Tax Control Account	0.00	534.97
2201	Purchase Tax Control Accoun	459.34	0.00
3200	Profit and Loss Account	0.00	0.00
			3124.73

Save   Print   Delete   Close

3 Click Print.

4 Select period.

Criteria	
Criteria	
	To
Period	Month 12, December 1999
	OK Cancel

5 Click OK.

The Budget Report

You can amend your nominal account Budget values at any time by using the Global Changes feature from the Tools menu.

The Budget Report displays the current values in your purchases, sales, direct expenses and overhead account codes for the months you select and the year-to-date. Use this report to see how your business actually traded compared with the monthly budget you set against the nominal ledger accounts for the chosen months and the year to date.

1 Click Budgets from the Financials toolbar.

2 In the Criteria box enter the From and To Period required.

3 Select Default Layout of Accounts (1).

When you run a year end, Sage Line 50 offers you the option to move the actual monthly values for the year just ended to the budgets for the coming year. This sets the budget values to be what really happened in each month of the year just ended. You can also add a percentage increase to your budget values to reflect any anticipated rise in sales, purchases, costs, etc. for the coming year.

4 Ensure Preview is selected.

5 Click OK to generate the report.

6 To print, click Print, then OK.

7 Click Close.

The Prior Year Report

Use the Prior Year report to compare your current trading results against how you did for the same period last year.

The Prior Year report compares the current values in your purchases, sales, direct expenses and overhead accounts codes using the formats as set up for you in your chart of accounts. Trading activities are detailed for both the current month and the year-to-date, or alternatively for any period you specify.

This report compares how your business is trading for the specified period against the same period in the previous year. Year-to-date totals and ratios are also included. To produce a Prior Year report, from the Financials window do the following:

1 Click Prior Yr to bring up the Criteria box.

2 Select Period required here.

3 Select Default Layout of Accounts (1).

To make a Prior Year Adjustment for your business refer to the Sage Line 50 Help Library Topics and search for Prior Year.

4 Check Output is set to Preview.

5 Click OK to continue.

6 To print, click Print, then OK.

7 Click Close.

The VAT Return

Use the Wizard button to guide you through the VAT Return process.

For businesses that need to submit VAT Return forms to HM Customs & Excise, Sage Line 50 provides all the features to enable you to do this quickly and accurately, calculating both input and output tax for you from the information you have entered over the period. This is a prime reason for keeping accurate accounts.

Input tax is the VAT you are charged on your business purchases and expenses. Output tax is the VAT your business charges on its taxable supplies or services. Because Value Added Tax is a tax charged to the final consumer, a business needs to calculate what input tax can be reclaimed and how much output tax needs paying to Customs & Excise. This is the purpose of the VAT Return.

Before reconciling your VAT transactions, you should back up your data files. Reconciling your transactions sets a flag against each transaction so it is automatically excluded from subsequent VAT Returns.

You have the facility to set up 99 tax codes, but on installation Sage Line 50 sets the standard UK and EC VAT rates for you, so you will probably not have to change anything. The default is set to the standard rate T1, presently at 17.5%, whilst others you may need are T0 (zero-rated) and T9 (transactions not involving VAT).

Within the nominal ledger are three accounts, namely the Sales Tax Control account (2200), Purchase Tax Control account (2201) and VAT liability account (2202). An accumulated total appears in the Sales account for the output tax charged to your customers whilst another accumulated total appears in the Purchase account for the input tax charged to your business.

The Audit Trail VAT column shows whether a transaction is reconciled or not. R = reconciled; N = unreconciled; a hyphen (-) or a dash (–) = a non-VAT transaction.

When your VAT Return is due, enter the correct date range into the system and the program will calculate the difference between the input and output tax and will inform you of the net VAT due to either the Customs & Excise or yourselves.

After reconciling your VAT Return, VAT on the Sales and Purchases Control accounts for this VAT period need transferring to the VAT Liability nominal account. When a bank payment to the Customs & Excise is made or received, the VAT Liability account is cleared, leaving a zero balance.

...cont'd

Ensure all transactions have been reconciled and the Audit Trail checked before running your VAT Return.

Use the Wizard button to guide you through the VAT Return process.

Use the Calculate button to automatically calculate the totals for your VAT Return.

Three reports are available for printing: Detailed, Summary and the VAT Return. The Detailed and Summary reports give a breakdown of all the totals from each box on the VAT Return.

To produce your VAT Return

1 From the Financials window click VAT to bring up the VAT Return window displaying zero totals.

2 Enter the inclusive VAT period dates here.

Value Added Tax Return

Wizard Training Limited
Wizard House
10 High Street
Anytown

For the period | 01/10/1999
to | 31/12/1999

VAT due in this period on sales	1	534.97
VAT due in this period on EC acquisitions	2	0.00
Total VAT due (sum of boxes 1 and 2)	3	534.97
VAT reclaimed in this period on purchases	4	227.51
Net VAT to be paid to Customs or reclaimed by you	5	307.46
Total value of sales, excluding VAT	6	3056.91
Total value of purchases, excluding VAT	7	1299.99
Total value of EC sales, excluding VAT	8	0.00
Total value of EC purchases, excluding VAT	9	0.00

Calculate   Reconcile   Print   ☐ Include Reconciled   ℹ   Close

3 Click Calculate to calculate totals for this return. You will be informed if any unreconciled transactions have been found.

4 Click on a VAT total for a breakdown.

VAT Breakdown - VAT due on Sales

VAT due in this period on sales | 1 | 534.97

T/C	Sales Invoices	Sales Credits	Receipts	Journal Credits	
T0	0.00	0.00	0.00	0.00
T1	534.97	0.00	0.00	0.00
T2	0.00	0.00	0.00	0.00
T3	0.00	0.00	0.00	0.00
T4	0.00	0.00	0.00	0.00
T5	0.00	0.00	0.00	0.00
	534.97	0.00	0.00	0.00

Close

5 Double-click on T/C for a transaction breakdown.

6 Close each window to return to VAT Return.

VAT Breakdown - Transactions

Tax Code : | T1 | Sales Invoices - VAT

No	A/C	Date	Details	Amount
12	4000	28/10/1999		188.93
13	4000	15/11/1999		82.00
14	4000	27/10/1999		141.70
15	4000	10/11/1999		61.56
33	4000	05/12/1999	Automatic Kettle	18.99
34	4000	05/12/1999	Waste Bin - Floral	41.04
35	4000	05/12/1999	Adhesive	0.77

Close   Total : | 534.97

7 Click Print, Run and OK to print the return.

...cont'd

Check that the balance of your VAT Return agrees with the balance of your VAT Control Accounts.

Use the VAT Transfer Wizard to transfer money from the Sales and Purchase Tax Control accounts to the VAT Liability account.

Sage Line 50 already has the following tax rates set up:

T0 = zero rated transactions.

T1 = standard rate.

T4 = sales to customers in EC.

T7 = zero rated purchases from suppliers in EC.

T8 = standard rated purchases from suppliers in EC.

T9 = transactions not involving VAT.

The VAT Transfer Wizard

Use the VAT Transfer Wizard to guide you through the transfer of your VAT liability once you have successfully reconciled and printed your VAT return.

1 From the Sage Line 50 toolbar select Wizards, then click VAT Transfer Wizard.

2 Click Yes to confirm you wish to continue.

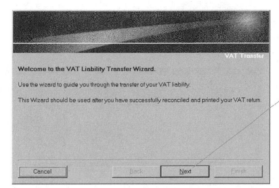

3 Click Next to proceed with the Wizard.

4 Work your way through each screen entering details where required and clicking Next until you reach the Confirm Posting Details window.

5 Click Finish to confirm details or Cancel to abandon.

Financial Reports

Sage Line 50 offers a wide range of Financial Reports that provide management information to enable effective decision making, planning and forecasting.

New to Sage Line 50 – You can now calculate profit and loss for the current month or for any range of consecutive months within your current financial year.

A considerable number of reports are set up at installation time, but many can be customised if required for your business by changing the appearance of the layout, the font type or by adding/removing certain text. Refer to Chapter Twelve for more details. To generate a report:

1 From the Financials toolbar click Reports.

2 Select the report layout required.

3 Check Output is set to Preview.

4 Click Run to view the report.

The grouping and positioning of nominal codes on the Financial Reports is determined by the Chart of Account.

5 Enter appropriate Criteria here.

6 Click OK to generate the report.

Information used for creating Financial Reports is taken from the actuals column in the Nominal Ledger Record.

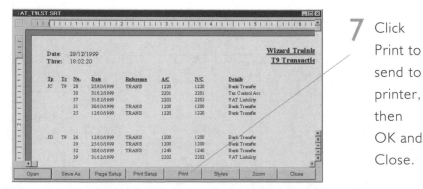

7 Click Print to send to printer, then OK and Close.

Fixed Assets

This Chapter explains how to work with Fixed Asset Records and how to view the value of your assets by running Fixed Asset Reports. It also details the three accepted methods of depreciation offered by Sage Line 50, enabling you to decide which is the most appropriate method to use for your business.

Covers

The Fixed Assets Toolbar | 134

Recording your Fixed Assets | 135

Fixed Asset Depreciation | 137

Depreciation and Valuation | 138

Chapter Eleven

The Fixed Assets Toolbar

This toolbar features options for creating Fixed Asset Records and setting up the method of depreciation, performing valuation of Fixed Assets and the generation of your Fixed Asset reports.

 To Create a Fixed Asset Record.

 To Report on Asset Valuation.

 To Run Fixed Asset Reports.

Recording your Fixed Assets

Have the following information ready before entering your Fixed Asset Records; purchase date of asset and cost price, depreciation method and rate, depreciation balance sheet nominal code and depreciation profit and loss nominal code.

Fixed Assets can be divided into 99 different categories for analysis and reporting purposes. Use the Fixed Asset Categories option from the Settings menu to add/edit a category.

See Default Layout of Accounts (COA) for the five Fixed Asset Category Accounts already set up.

Fixed Assets are items such as office equipment, buildings, machinery, etc. owned by the business. Their depreciation is an expense and can be offset against profits.

However, before recording Fixed Asset information, it is important that the correct method and rate of depreciation be decided upon and applied consistently. Different classes of Fixed Assets are often depreciated at different rates, for example, office furniture may be depreciated at a different rate to motor vehicles.

Sage Line 50 offers the choice of three depreciation methods: Straight Line, Reducing Balance and Write Off. For the Straight Line method, the asset is depreciated by a fixed percentage (calculated from the original Cost Price of the asset) every month until the asset is reduced to zero. For the Reducing Balance method, the asset is depreciated again monthly by a fixed percentage, but this time the percentage is applied to the new book value of the asset.

The last method, Write Off depreciation, makes one last posting to depreciate the remaining value of the asset.

When ready to enter your fixed assets for the first time you will notice that the Fixed Assets window is empty. As soon as Fixed Asset Records are entered, they will be displayed one record per line. To bring up the Fixed Assets window:

1 Click Assets from the Sage Line 50 toolbar.

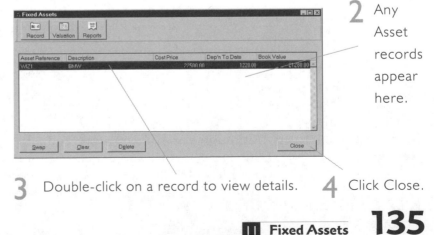

2 Any Asset records appear here.

3 Double-click on a record to view details.

4 Click Close.

Adding Fixed Asset Records.

The first time you use the Assets option, the Fixed Assets window will be empty. To add a Fixed Asset record, have all the necessary information to hand, then do the following:

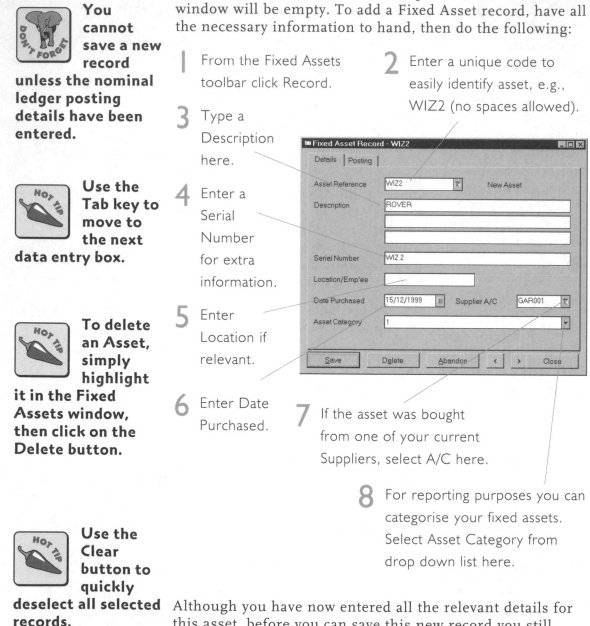

You cannot save a new record unless the nominal ledger posting details have been entered.

Use the Tab key to move to the next data entry box.

To delete an Asset, simply highlight it in the Fixed Assets window, then click on the Delete button.

1 From the Fixed Assets toolbar click Record.

2 Enter a unique code to easily identify asset, e.g., WIZ2 (no spaces allowed).

3 Type a Description here.

4 Enter a Serial Number for extra information.

5 Enter Location if relevant.

6 Enter Date Purchased.

7 If the asset was bought from one of your current Suppliers, select A/C here.

8 For reporting purposes you can categorise your fixed assets. Select Asset Category from drop down list here.

Use the Clear button to quickly deselect all selected records.

Although you have now entered all the relevant details for this asset, before you can save this new record you still need to enter the appropriate nominal ledger posting details. This is explained on the next two pages.

Fixed Asset Depreciation

The Fixed Asset option does not post depreciation for you, only records the asset and current value. Use Month End option to automatically make monthly depreciation postings.

Once you have saved a record, the depreciation method can only ever be changed to Write Off.

Once a depreciation posting has been made by the Month End/Year End routines for this asset, the Cost Price or Book Value cannot be changed.

The Posting Tab is used for entering the necessary nominal ledger posting details. Then, when you run the Month End/Year End depreciation posting routines, asset depreciation will be added to the appropriate account code as an expense to your business and will be shown on the balance sheet and profit and loss report.

There are four depreciation accounts already set up in the balance sheet of the nominal ledger by Sage Line 50. Every time an asset is depreciated, the amount of depreciation is posted as a credit posting. Codes include 0021 (Plant/Machinery Depreciation), 0031 (Office Equipment Depreciation), 0041 (Furniture/Fixture Depreciation) and 0051 (Motor Vehicles Depreciation).

Similarly, four depreciation accounts are already set up for you in the profit & loss section of the nominal ledger. Every time an asset is depreciated, the value of that depreciation is added to the account code as an expense to the company (debit posting). Codes include 8001 (Plant/Machinery Depreciation), 8002 (Furniture/Fitting Depreciation), 8003 (Vehicle Depreciation) and 8004 (Office Equipment Depreciation).

You need to enter the annual rate of depreciation. For the Straight Line method, the value entered will be divided by twelve to calculate the monthly depreciation. For example, to depreciate an asset completely over five years using the straight line method, the Dep'n Rate would be 20%, depreciating at 1.666% monthly until after five years the book value is zero. So, for an item costing £15,000, a depreciation value of £250 would be posted for 60 months.

Where Book Value details are required, then enter the current book value. If the asset is brand new, this should be the same as the Cost Price. If an asset has already been depreciated, then enter the cost price minus depreciation. If the reducing balance method was selected, the Book Value will be used to calculate the depreciation amount. Sage Line 50 will automatically reduce this value by the depreciation amount during the month end procedure.

Depreciation and Valuation

Setting up a Fixed Asset depreciation posting

From the Fixed Assets window, click the Valuation button to quickly check the total cost, total current book value and the total amount of depreciation that has taken place so far on all of your asset records.

1 After entering the Fixed Asset Record details (page 136) select the Posting tab.

2 Select Department where appropriate.

3 Enter nominal ledger balance sheet account code.

4 Enter nominal ledger profit and loss account code.

5 Select Depreciation Method here.

6 Enter annual percentage rate of depreciation.

7 Enter Cost Price (Net) here.

8 Enter the current Book Value.

To run a Fixed Asset report, click Reports from the Fixed Assets toolbar and select one of the ready set up reports included with Sage Line 50.

9 Click Save to store details.

10 Click Close.

Valuation of Fixed Assets

To see details about the current value of your assets including total cost, previous total depreciation and total current book value do the following:

1 From the Fixed Assets window click Valuation to bring up the Asset Valuation window.

2 When finished, click Close.

The Report Designer

This chapter shows you how to create a new report and also how to edit an existing report to meet your own requirements. Report Designer is very powerful and provides options for grouping and sorting information, adding calculations such as totals, setting up criteria and filters to search for information as well as designing the layout and format of the report.

Covers

Introducing the Report Designer | 140

Creating a new Report | 141

Modifying an existing Report | 144

Chapter Twelve

Introducing the Report Designer

For more details about the Report Designer, click Reports from the Sage Line 50 toolbar and press F1.

When you first install Sage Line 50, you can immediately generate and print all of the reports and stationery to suit most business needs. If you use stationery supplied by Sage, the data should fit in the pre-printed stationery forms without adjustment.

There will be occasions though when you need a new report not already supplied, or you need to modify an existing one to suit your specific needs. The Report Designer lets you do all of this to meet any specific requirements that you have.

You may need to click on the right scroll button on the Sage Line 50 toolbar a few times to bring the Report button into view, depending on the screen area setting for your computer.

The Report Designer, although an integral part of Sage Line 50, is actually a complete windows application on its own. The Designer has its own Title Bar, Menu Bar, and Desktop area on which you can open multiple document windows. Each document window can hold an entirely separate layout file, which means you can work on several layouts at once, if you wish. To run Report Designer:

1 Select the Report button from the Sage Line 50 toolbar.

2 The Report Designer window appears.

3 Click here on each folder to see a list of existing layouts.

Use Report Designer to design new (or modify existing) reports to fit into any new pre-printed stationery forms your business may adopt.

Report Designer
File View Help

Sage Line 50

Sage Line 50
  DEFAULTS
    DEFAULT.SLT
    DEFAULT.SLY
    DEFAULT.SRT
  DEMODATA
  LABELS
  LAYOUTS
  LETTERS
  REPORTS
  TEMPLATE
  Favourites

NUM

Creating a new Report

The following example shows you how to create a Customer Balance and Credit List for a single customer or a range of customers using the Report Wizard. The report contains the Customer's account reference, company name and account balance, together with their credit limit. The report is sorted to show the customer with the lowest balance first. The report also displays a balance total.

When the Wizard is finished the Report Designer appears with the new report/layout open ready for you to work on or preview.

| From the Sage Line 50 toolbar select Reports.

2 Click File and New from the Report Designer menu.

3 Select Customer option.

4 Click Next to continue.

5 Enter report Title here.

When your new report is complete, you can either save, preview, or print it.

6 Click Next.

7 The next screen confirms your selection. Click Next to progress to selecting report variables.

You can also double-click the required variable to copy it to the Report Variables view.

8 Select variable required from this list.

9 Click single right arrow button to copy to Report Variables view.

10 Repeat Step 9 for all required variables.

11 Click Next.

To make a selective choice of variables, hold down the CTRL key whilst clicking on variables required. Click the > button to transfer them as a group.

12 Grouping is not required, so just click Next.

13 Select SALES_ LEDGER.BALANCE.

14 Click > button.

15 Click Next.

16 Select and move SALES_LEDGER .BALANCE to Total Variables.

17 Click Next.

 To highlight a range of variables, hold down the SHIFT key and click the first and last variable in the list. Select the > button to transfer the range as a group.

18 Set Status to Enabled for Customer Ref and Tran Date.

19 Click Finish to generate report layout.

 Should you ever need to transfer all the available variables simply click the >> button.

The Report Designer now generates the appropriate report layout for you. You will be able to see how the layout is divided into sections, i.e., Page Header, Details, Page Footer, etc.

If the layout is not as required, you can modify the report later. First you need to check that it provides the information you require by running a report preview.

...cont'd

Previewing your Report

Maximise your report layout window to view all the variables.

Your report will appear in your Customers Reports window after saving.

1 Click Preview to run your new report.

2 The Criteria box appears.

3 Enter Criteria details.

Be careful not to overwrite any existing reports. They may be useful to you later.

4 Click OK to run the report.

6 To close, click on File and Exit.

5 To save, select Save As from File menu, enter a filename and click OK.

Modifying an existing Report

To remove your company's name and address from all your layout files, select Company Preferences from the Settings menu on the Sage Line 50 toolbar. De-select the option by clicking the Print Name and Address on Stationery check box and click OK.

The Report Designer lets you modify existing report layout files and default reports supplied with the program. These will, however, need saving under a new filename.

As an example, you can modify the report just created and saved to include only customers with a balance greater than £1000. This is called a filter, which is embedded in the report layout. To make these changes it is easier to start from the Sage Line 50 Customers option:

1 From the Customer toolbar click on the Reports option.

2 Select your report from the list and click Edit.

3 Click Format, Filter.

4 In the Filter box click Build.

You can edit a Fixed Report and save it to a new filename. The original report remains unchanged and your new report is added to the list.

If you make a mistake designing the report, select immediately the Edit Undo option from the Edit menu.

7 Click OK, Preview & Save.

5 Select Sales_Ledger.Credit_Limit and click Add.

6 Click > and type 1000 here, then OK.

Opening Balances

This chapter explains how to enter opening balances for your customer, supplier, nominal and bank accounts as well as your products.

Covers

Introduction | 146

Opening Balances – Standard VAT | 147

Opening Balances – VAT Cash Accounting | 148

Clearing Opening Balances from Trial Balance | 149

Entering Balances Part Way through the Year | 151

Nominal Ledger and Bank Account | 152

Opening Balances for Products | 154

Chapter Thirteen

Introduction

Print off a copy of the Opening Balances checklist from the F1 Help system to guide you.

Posted Opening Balances for your customers and suppliers are displayed in the trial balance report, which needs clearing before entering Opening Balances for the nominal ledger account, bank account and products.

These are the Nominal Codes used in the Trial Balance:

1100 = Debtors Control Account

2100 = Creditors Control Account

9998 = Suspense Account.

It is important to set up opening balances correctly and in the right order. All accounts remain at zero until you enter opening balances for your Customers, Suppliers, Nominal, Bank and Products.

Where opening balances are carried forward, accurate figures need entering to indicate the true financial position of the business, for example, its Debtors, Creditors, Nominal Ledger Trial Balance, as well as its Stock.

Standard VAT and VAT Cash Accounting

Standard VAT calculates the VAT return on the invoices/credits you have raised for your customers or received from your suppliers, and any bank/cash payments or receipts or journal entries with vatable tax codes.

Customer opening balances can be entered as lump sum balances. It is recommended, however, that each outstanding invoice and credit note be entered separately for cross referencing. Recording separate transactions will also provide accurate aged debtors analysis.

The second method, the VAT Cash Accounting scheme, is where the VAT return is calculated on the invoices/credits which you have received payment for from your customers or you have paid to your suppliers. Included too are any bank/cash payments or receipts or journal entries with vatable tax codes.

With VAT Cash Accounting each invoice and credit note must be entered for your customers individually, with the correct tax code.

The same Standard VAT and VAT Cash Accounting conditions apply for entering opening balances for suppliers. Again, it is recommended for Standard VAT that separate transactions be recorded for outstanding invoices and credit notes to match up with payments later instead of grouping them all together in one opening balance. Separate transactions will again provide accurate aged creditors information.

Opening Balances – Standard VAT

Follow the same procedures as for Customers when entering opening balances for your Suppliers.

With the Standard VAT accounting method opening balances can be entered as a lump sum or individual transactions. You set up your customer balances using the Customer Record, accessed by using the Customers button on the Sage Line 50 toolbar.

Where customer information exists already, you can refer to the Aged Debtors Analysis and Detailed Customer Activity reports for cross referencing purposes and for checking that opening balances are recorded accurately. The Aged Creditors and Detailed Supplier Activity reports are also available for your suppliers.

When entering a total for outstanding invoices/credit notes, O/BAL is a useful reference.

To enter customer Opening Balance details

1 From the Customers window click on the required record, then click Record on the toolbar.

By recording the original invoice/credit note date, you will have accurate details of overdue debtors.

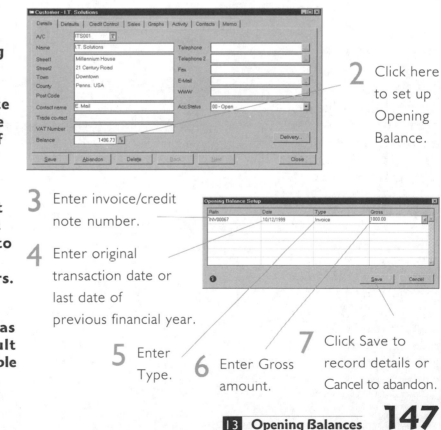

2 Click here to set up Opening Balance.

3 Enter invoice/credit note number.

4 Enter original transaction date or last date of previous financial year.

Use Next and Back buttons to move between customers.

T9 is set as the default non-vatable tax code.

5 Enter Type.

6 Enter Gross amount.

7 Click Save to record details or Cancel to abandon.

Opening Balances – VAT Cash Accounting

To enter Opening Balances for your suppliers, click on the Suppliers button, then follow the steps you would with Customers.

Using this particular scheme each customer invoice and credit note needs entering individually with the correct tax code because VAT is only considered when payment is being made. The opening balances can be entered via the Batch Invoices or Credits screens.

To enter customer Opening Balance details

1 From the Customers window click on the required record, then click Record on the toolbar.

Use Audit Trail from Financials to identify reference numbers.

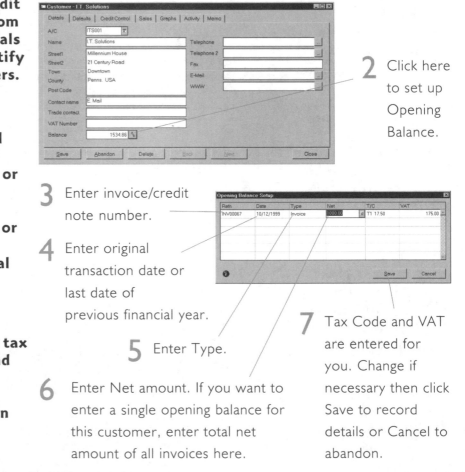

2 Click here to set up Opening Balance.

Enter original date of invoice or credit note for accurate aged debtors analysis or last date of previous financial year.

3 Enter invoice/credit note number.

4 Enter original transaction date or last date of previous financial year.

5 Enter Type.

The default tax code and VAT appear automatically, but can be changed if necessary.

6 Enter Net amount. If you want to enter a single opening balance for this customer, enter total net amount of all invoices here.

7 Tax Code and VAT are entered for you. Change if necessary then click Save to record details or Cancel to abandon.

Clearing Opening Balances from Trial Balance

Always print a copy of your Trial Balance report BEFORE clearing the opening balances.

When opening balances for your customers and suppliers are saved, they are posted to the trial balance. These entries need clearing or they will be duplicated when posting opening balances for your nominal ledger accounts. This will produce an incorrect balance sheet.

Before you start, make a note from your trial balance of the values of your Debtors and Creditors Control Accounts, your Sales Tax and Purchase Tax Control Accounts and your Suspense Account and whether each one is a debit or a credit, for example:

If you are using VAT Cash Accounting, balances need clearing in your Sales and Purchase Tax Control Accounts.

Trial Balance

Name	TC	Debit	Credit
Debtors Control Account	T9	30,687.19	
Creditors Control Account	T9		21,189.78
Suspense	T9		9,497.41
BALANCE		30,687.19	30,687.19

When entering journal entries into the transaction table, use opposite values from the trial balance, i.e., Debit (+) and Credit (-).

Once the relevant details have been noted, a Journal Entry from the Nominal Ledger needs to be made to clear the balances. Using the details from the above example, the entry would be as follows:

Journal Entry

Name	TC	Debit	Credit
Debtors Control Account	T9		30,687.19
Creditors Control Account	T9	21,189.78	
Suspense	T9	9,497.41	
BALANCE		30,687.19	30,687.19

The journal entry can only be saved when the value in the Balance box is zero.

...cont'd

Once you have noted what entries you need to make, you can add them to the Journal. When you process these entries, the opening balances in the Trial Balance will be cleared. To make the entries do the following:

 Always bear in mind that for a journal entry, VAT is neither calculated for you nor posted to the VAT control account.

1 From the Sage Line 50 toolbar click Nominal.

2 Click on Journals from the Nominal Ledger window to bring up the Journals window.

3 The Ref. entry is optional. Type a reference if desired.

4 Check for correct Date.

 Use the Finder button to quickly locate the correct codes.

Nominal Ledger Journals

Journals

	Ref		Date							Balance	
			01/01/2000							0.00	

N/C	Name	Dept	Details	Tc	Debit	Credit
1100	Debtors Control Account	0	Clear O/B	T9	0.00	30687.19
2100	Creditors Control Account	0	Clear O/B	T9	21189.78	0.00
9998	Suspense Account	0	Clear O/B	T9	9497.41	0.00
		0			0.00	0.00
					30687.19	30687.19

Save	Abandon	Memorise	Recall		Close

 If you make a mistake just click on the Abandon button and start again.

5 Enter details for both the credit and debits.

6 Note, the default Tax code of T9 is entered for you by Sage Line 50.

7 Check total Debit and Credit are equal and a zero balance is displayed in the Balance box.

8 Click Save to process your journal or Abandon to cancel.

9 Click Close to return to Nominal Ledger window.

Entering Balances Part Way through the Year

When you use Sage Line 50 for the first time and you set up Product records, this is also a good time to have a stock take so that you know the details you are entering are accurate. Sage Line 50 can only produce accurate reports if the information you enter is correct. This ia also a good time to check that Customer and Supplier details are still up to date.

Sage Line 50 needs Opening Balances in order to produce accurate financial statements. Because all accounts in all the ledgers have a zero balance when the program is first installed, it is important that the Opening Balances are entered as soon as possible. Without them your financial statements will not be accurate.

It is, however, quite possible to start using Sage Line 50 at any time through your financial year, and then enter the Opening Balances as they become available. For instance, if you have been in business for some time you will already have stock, products, customers and suppliers. You will have a transaction history. When you first start to use Sage Line 50 you will set up Records for your Customers, Suppliers, Products etc. This is when you can start to enter some Opening Balances.

If you do start to use Sage Line 50 part way through your financial year, you should contact your accountant as soon as possible for a detailed list showing all your outstanding Debtors and Creditors. You can then use this as the Opening Balances for your Customers and Suppliers.

You also need to ask for a Trial Balance from your accountant, which will give you the Opening Balances for each Nominal Ledger and Bank account.

You must at all times make sure that the information you enter is accurate. If you need to enter Opening Balances part way through your financial year, you will probably have a lot of Nominal Ledger opening balances to enter! It is important, therefore, that you enter these accurately otherwise your balance sheet will be incorrect.

You will also need to enter any year-to-date values from your Profit and Loss accounts. Your accountant should be able to provide you with this.

Nominal Ledger and Bank Account

If you have money in the bank or building society, their statement shows you have a balance under the credit column. They owe you that money, you are the creditor. When this money is recorded in your accounts, such asset balances are recorded the opposite way round as debits. If you have money in your bank or building society, the balance must be entered as a debit.

When entering opening balances for your Nominal Ledger or Bank account, double-entry postings are applied by Sage Line 50. For example, if you post a debit opening balance of £100 to your Building Society account (1220 by default), Sage Line 50 automatically posts £100 as a credit to your Suspense Account (9998 by default).

After you have entered all your Nominal Ledger and Bank account opening balances, the balance of the Suspense Account should be zero again. A new trial balance needs printing to check opening balances have been included for all your nominal accounts. If you still have a balance in your Suspense Account (i.e. it is not zero), an opening balance may have been omitted or a debit or credit misposted.

Nominal ledger opening balances

1 From the Sage Line 50 toolbar, select Nominal.

2 Click on the required account.

3 Click on the Record button.

Enter an opening balance for each nominal account code that appears on your trial balance.

4 Click the O/B button to enter the balance.

```
Nominal Record - Bank Deposit Account                    _ □ X
 Details | Graphs | Activity | Memo |
 N/C          1210        ▼
 Name         Bank Deposit Account
 Balance      0.00      %   Account Type   Bank Account

 Month        Actuals       Budgets        Prior Yr
 B/F          0.00          0.00           0.00
 Jan          0.00          0.00           0.00
 Feb          0.00          0.00           0.00
 Mar          0.00          0.00           0.00
 Apr          0.00          0.00           0.00
 May          0.00          0.00           0.00
 Jun          0.00          0.00           0.00
 Jul          0.00          0.00           0.00

   Save      Abandon      Delete      Back      Next      Close
```

5 Enter opening balance details here.

```
Opening Balance Setup                                      X
    Ref          Date          Debit          Credit
  O/Bal       10/12/1999      100.00          0.00
  ⓘ              Save          Cancel
```

6 Click Save, then Close.

Bank Opening Balances

You can also set up a Bank account Opening Balance directly from the Bank Record. To do this follow these steps:

> **You can enter Bank account opening balances either through the Bank Record or through the Nominal Ledger Record, but not both.**

1 From the Sage Line 50 toolbar, select Bank.

2 Click on the Bank Record you wish to set up an Opening Balance for and click on Record.

Bank Record

| Account Details | Bank Details | Contact | Activity | Memo |

A/C Ref 1220
Nominal Name Building Society Account
Current Balance 0.00
Minimum Limit 0.00
A/C Type Cheque Account
Currency 1 Pound Sterling
☐ No Bank Reconciliation

Save   Abandon   Delete   Close

> **An asset should always have a debit entry, whilst a liability should always have a credit entry.**

3 Click the O/B button to bring up the Opening Balance Setup box.

Opening Balance Setup

Ref O/Bal
Date 10/12/1999
Receipt 200.00
Payment 0.00

Save   Cancel

4 Enter Date if different from default date.

5 Enter opening balance as a Receipt or Payment. If you have money in your bank, this will be a Receipt.

6 Click Save to record the Opening balance information.

Opening Balances for Products

If you have selected the Ignore Stock Levels check box, you cannot enter an opening balance for this product.

When you create a Product Record, you will probably enter an Opening Balance for that product if you already have some in stock. However, there will be times when you need to enter an Opening Balance at a later date to that when the Record was set up.

If you do the latter, when you save the Opening Balance for a product, Sage Line 50 posts an Adjustment In transaction, which appears on the product reports. The valuation report will show the opening stock quantity at the cost price entered. To set up a Product Opening Balance:

If you select more than one Product Record, use the Back and Next buttons to move through them in turn.

1 From the Sage Line 50 toolbar, click Products.

2 Select the Product or products requiring an opening balance.

3 Click Record.

4 Click O/B button on the In Stock box.

Do not forget to enter the Cost Price for the Product when you set up the Opening Balance.

5 Enter Opening Balance details here.

6 Click Save to return to the Products Record, then Close.

Data Management

This chapter shows you important routines and procedures you need to use regularly for taking care of your data. Often data entered into the system is lost or corrupted by not following simple file maintenance. Backing up of data is essential to any business as problems often occur at the most inconvenient and crucial times.

Covers

Backing up Data | 156

Restoring Data | 157

Changing Global Values | 158

Importing Data | 160

File Maintenance | 162

Write Off, Refund and Return | 165

Posting Contra Entries | 168

Run Period End Functions | 169

Clearing the Audit Trail and Stock | 172

Chapter Fourteen

Backing up Data

Regular data backup (at least once daily) is essential in case of system error, when valuable data can be corrupted and sometimes lost. If this happens, you can at least restore important data files, reports and/or layout templates from your most up-to-date backup. A backup routine is provided by Sage Line 50 to automatically backup to your computer's Floppy Drive A:, but this can be changed to save to any drive and/or directory you require.

Backing up procedures vary from business to business; some use five disks for Monday to Friday and repeat their usage the following week. The important thing is to backup your data at least once a day! Sage Line 50 always prompts you to back up when you Exit the program, but to perform a backup at any other time, do the following:

1 From the Sage Line 50 menu, click on File.

2 Click on Backup.

3 To backup to Sage Line 50's default Drive A, click OK; else, to save to another drive or directory, follow steps 4–7.

4 To change backup destination, click Setup.

5 Select correct drive.

7 Click OK, then OK in the Backup Data Files dialog.

6 Select directory if appropriate.

Restoring Data

It is always advisable to run the Check Data option from File, Maintenance after you have restored your data.

Hopefully you should never have to restore your files, but should you be unlucky and suffer data loss or corruption, the Restore procedure allows you to revert to a previous backup. Which backup you restore from is up to you, but it will normally be the most recent.

The Restore facility allows data from your backup disks to replace your old data by erasing it and starting again. It is therefore very important to correctly label disks when you take a backup, and always keep them in a safe place. You may even consider keeping them somewhere other than on the premises in case of fire or theft!

Restoring data will erase the current Sage Line 50 data and replace it with data from your backup disks.

Because the restore procedure erases your old data, any data you entered since the backup is lost and will need entering again. Make sure that the Restore is first necessary, then do the following:

You must restore ALL your data, not just selective data files or a mismatch may exist between the ledger data, causing data corruption.

1 From the Sage Line 50 menu, click on File.

2 Click on Restore.

File

Open Demo Data

Backup...
Restore...

Import...

Maintenance...

Send Mail...

Log Off

Run Easy Startup Wizard

Exit

Restore Data Files   ☒

Restore

WARNING !
Restoring data from disk will overwrite your current data permanently.
If you are in any doubt, choose CANCEL now, then backup your existing data before proceeding.

Backup data is about to be restored from:
Drive A:

If restoring from a floppy disk, please ensure that the disk is in the drive before you begin.

If you wish to change the source of the Restore, then select the Setup button.

[Setup]   [OK]   [Cancel]

3 Click OK to restore data files, by default, from Drive A:, else go to Step 4.

4 If you are restoring from a Drive other than A:, click Setup, select location, then click OK to return to this box.

5 Click OK to perform the restore.

Changing Global Values

Use the Global Changes option to alter the values for either all or for a selected group of accounts or products.

Certain values in Sage Line 50, such as Credit Limits, have applications throughout the program. From time to time certain record values may need changing for all your records or for a selected group. To save time, these values can be changed quickly and easily by using the Global Changes Wizard. The Wizard guides you with on-screen instructions to make the necessary changes where required.

Values within the customer, supplier and nominal ledger records can be changed as well as certain values within your product records, for example the product sales price could be increased globally by 5% or the re-order level increased for a range of products. To run the Wizard:

Click on the Back button at any time to check what you entered in the previous screen or Cancel to abandon your changes.

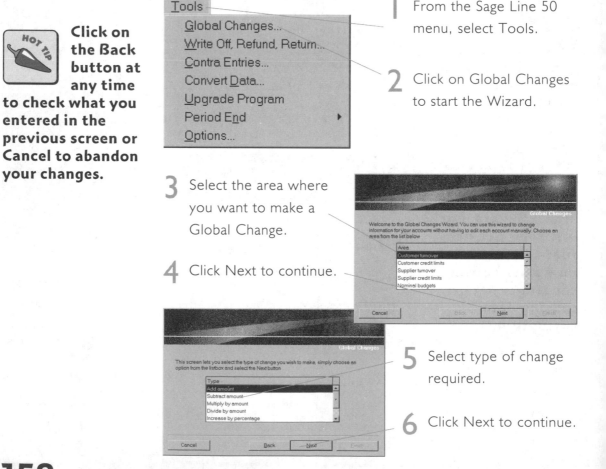

1 From the Sage Line 50 menu, select Tools.

2 Click on Global Changes to start the Wizard.

3 Select the area where you want to make a Global Change.

4 Click Next to continue.

5 Select type of change required.

6 Click Next to continue.

...cont'd

To exit from a wizard at any point, choose the Cancel button or press ALT + F4.

7 You must enter a value here before Sage Line 50 will let you progress.

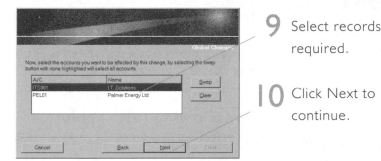

8 Click Next to continue.

Use the Global Changes Wizard to quickly set up Discount Rates, Re-order Levels and Re-order Quantities for your Products.

9 Select records required.

10 Click Next to continue.

Always check you have entered the correct information as you may not be able to easily undo changes.

11 Check that the details are correct. If you need to make any changes, use the Back button until you get to the appropriate screen, make the changes, then keep clicking Next to get back to this screen.

12 Click Finish to action the changes.

Whilst the Global Changes Wizard allows you to make changes quickly and easily, be very careful when using it and always double-check your values because when you click Finish, the changes you have entered are immediately actioned. In some cases these are quite major changes, such as increasing all product sales prices by a stated percentage. If you were to accidentally enter the wrong percentage, you cannot easily undo the resulting price changes!

Importing Data

A unit of data in a record can be one of the following data types: Text, e.g. AßCd234, Integer, e.g. 10,20,30,40, Decimal Number, e.g. 25.3,145.05, 0.90.

It can be very laborious entering a lot of data into certain records so Sage Line 50 lets you import data into the following record types – customers, suppliers, products and nominal ledger – provided it conforms to the correct file format. A group of new records can be created and imported directly into Sage Line 50 or existing records updated with new details, replacing records being entering individually.

The text can be produced using any program which allows you to save the file in text format (.txt), for example, a word processing, spreadsheet or accounts package. The text must be in a specific format otherwise it will not be imported correctly and errors will be reported. These files are called CSV files (Comma Separated Values).

Avoid import errors by not exceeding maximum data unit length and using the correct data type, e.g., do not enter a decimal number into a integer data unit.

The following rules apply:

A comma separates each unit of data, i.e. B01,Bolt,100,0.2

Each data record takes up a single line.

Each data record is terminated by pressing ENTER.

Any spaces at the start or end of a data unit are ignored, but spaces within data units are included.

Use quotes to include commas within a data unit, i.e. "25, Bell Lane"

Each data unit in a record must be entered in strict order to avoid being imported incorrectly.

When importing account code data of customers and suppliers records, it is converted to upper-case and restricted to eight characters. Blank spaces are removed.

Two consecutive commas (,,) will move to the next data unit.

An example of three typical CSV data records:

1,SI,BROWN,4000,2,Supplies,03/10/99,,27.15,T1,Y

2,SC,WHITE,4000,2,Credit,14/10/99,,35.00,T1,N

3,PI,BLACK,5000,4,Equipment,25/11/99,,52.50,T1,Y

...cont'd

To Import a Data File

1 From the Sage Line 50 menu, select File.

A SPACE between two commas (, ,) causes the existing data to be erased.

2 Click Import.

3 Click on correct Import Type here.

4 Click Run to continue.

Importing a blank unit of data does not overwrite existing data – it leaves it intact and forces a move to the next data unit. Use this feature for changing only selected data in a record.

5 Select Drive or Directory to Import from.

6 Enter Name of File to Import or select from list.

7 Click OK.

File
Open Demo Data
Backup...
Restore...
Import...
Maintenance...
Send Mail...
Log Off
Run Easy Startup Wizard
Exit

File Import
Import Type
⦿ Customer Records   ◯ Stock Records
◯ Supplier Records   ◯ Stock Transactions
◯ Nominal Ledger Records
◯ Transactions
                              Run   Close

Open
File name:
*.CSV
List files of type:
CSV files (*.CSV)

Folders:
c:\line50
📁 c:\
📁 line50
   📁 accdata
   📁 bitmaps
   📁 criteria
   📁 defaults
   📁 demodata
   📁 html
Drives:
💾 c: win98

OK
Cancel
Network...

File Maintenance

The Check Data option should be used on a daily basis to check for errors, so they can be quickly detected and rectified.

Sage Line 50 provides four important options to manage and check the validity of your data files. These features include checking for input errors, allowing manual data error corrections, data compression and building new data files.

Error Checking

You should use the Check Data facility to check the validity of your data files. If necessary you can then make corrections where required. This facility needs to be run regularly, before making backups and after restoring data.

If there are problems whilst checking the data, a File Maintenance Problem Report dialog box appears which includes a Summary, Comments, Errors or Warnings.

To print out an error report, select the category tab required from the File Maintenance Problems Report dialog box and click the Print button.

1   From the Sage Line 50 menu, select File.

2   Click Maintenance.

3   From the File maintenance window click Check Data.

4   Checking Data Files box shows the progress.

5   Check out details using Tabs.

6   Click Fix to correct errors, else Close.

...cont'd

The reference field can be amended in the Edit Transaction Allocation Record.

Use the Edit button to amend any reference for payments or receipts made against a transaction.

Use the Find button to search for transactions.

Journal entries cannot be amended using the Edit button. To do so select the Journals option from the Nominal Ledger toolbar and make the necessary adjustment by posting a journal entry with the opposite values.

Correcting Transactions

Any mistakes made while entering transactions can be corrected using the Corrections option from the File Maintenance window. These transactions, however, can only be edited or deleted if they are still held in the Audit Trail. To correct a transaction:

1 Click Corrections from the File Maintenance window.

2 Select transaction to correct.

3 Click Edit.

4 For changes to the customer/supplier account, bank, details, reference or date make your corrections here.

5 For more changes click Edit.

6 To change the nominal account, details, department, amount or VAT amount/code, make your corrections here.

7 Close and Save.

If an amendment cannot be posted, a warning will appear detailing why not.

Reversing VAT Reconciled Transactions

You can delete a transaction provided it has not been reconciled on the VAT Return. However, any VAT reconciled transaction will display a Reverse button instead of the Delete button in the Transaction Record window. To reverse VAT reconciliation on a transaction:

After confirming a reversal of VAT reconciliation, the Ref entry in the Posting Errors Corrections box reads 'Cancel'.

1 From the Posting Error Corrections window, select transaction and click Edit.

2 To reverse VAT reconciliation click on the Reverse button.

3 Click Yes to confirm.

Data Compression

Make sure you take a back up of your data files BEFORE running Compress Data as the action is irreversible.

When there has been a lot of activity, such as deletion or amendments of any records, use the Compress Data option to produce a new set of data files. Sage Line 50 will then reduce file size by removing these deleted records, freeing up disk space. To perform data compression, do this:

1 Click Compress Data from the File Maintenance Box.

2 Click Compress.

3 Click Close.

Take care when using the Rebuild option as it will clear the contents of your existing data files. USE WITH CAUTION.

Rebuild

This Sage Line 50 option is for creating a new or selected set of data files. From the File Maintenance window:

1 Click Rebuild to run option.

2 Select files to rebuild and click OK.

Write Off, Refund and Return

Sage Line 50 procedures for these functions vary depending on whether you are using the Standard VAT Scheme or VAT Cash Accounting. Refer to Help Topics for more information.

Use these options to carry out accounting procedures that affect your customer and supplier accounts, e.g. cheque returns, invoice refunds and outstanding invoice transactions. How you record these depends on your VAT method.

Refunds

Use this facility for credit notes, payments on account and invoices where a money refund is required rather than a replacement of goods or provision of services. If you are using the Standard VAT Scheme, do the following:

1 From the Sage Line 50 menu, click Tools.

For VAT Cash Accounting the transaction needs writing off manually. For more information, refer to Recording Refunds (VAT Cash Accounting) section of the Sage Line 50 Help.

2 Click Write Off, Refund, Return...

3 Select Ledger required, e.g. Purchase Ledger.

4 Click Next.

5 Select where you want to make the amendments.

6 Click Next.

To find out if you are able to reclaim VAT paid on a Write Off, contact HM Customs & Excise.

7 Select the account to make the invoice refund to.

8 Click Next to continue.

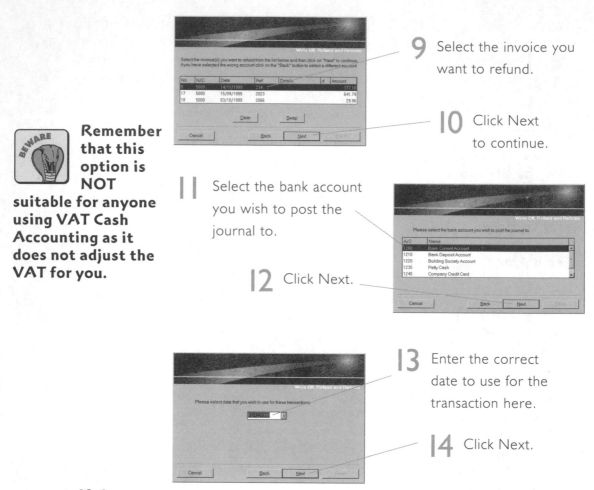

9 Select the invoice you want to refund.

10 Click Next to continue.

Remember that this option is NOT suitable for anyone using VAT Cash Accounting as it does not adjust the VAT for you.

11 Select the bank account you wish to post the journal to.

12 Click Next.

13 Enter the correct date to use for the transaction here.

14 Click Next.

If the presented summary of information is incorrect, use the Back button to return to the appropriate box and modify.

15 The information you have entered is shown in this summary.

16 Check carefully that it is all correct. Use the Back button if you need to make any change, else go to Step 17.

17 Click Finish to post the transaction to your ledgers.

...cont'd

Using a credit note to refund an outstanding customer invoice is known as allocating the credit note to the customer invoice.

When a sales credit note is posted to the customer's account it has the same reference as the refunded invoice.

To record a refund using the Write Off, Refund and Return Wizard, the refund must need fully refunding and must not have been removed from the audit trail. If it has been removed or you need to make a partial refund, you must use the manual refund method.

Write Off

At times a customer will not or cannot pay an outstanding debt, so the amount can be written off to a bad debt account. The steps are very similar to a Refund, but fewer. Just select the appropriate Write Off for Step 5 (page 165) and follow the simple instructions.

Cheque Returns

Occasionally you may need to record a cheque from a customer that you wish to cancel or that the bank has returned. If you use the Standard VAT Scheme, do this:

1 From the Sage Line 50 menu, click Tools.

2 Click Write Off, Refund, Return.

3 Select ledger & click Next.

4 Click Cheque Returns and Next.

5 Select account, click Next.

6 Select cheque & carry out Steps 12–17 on Page 166.

Posting Contra Entries

Use the Audit Trail for viewing transactions, as well as Customer and Supplier activity.

Where you have a customer who is also one of your suppliers, you may offset sales invoices against your supplier's purchase invoices. To do this, you use the Contra Entries option from the Tools menu to match one or more sales invoices with your purchase invoices. Sage Line 50 will then automatically update the appropriate ledgers. To post a Contra Entry:

If VAT Cash Accounting is being used, make sure the selected transactions have matching tax codes.

1 From the Sage Line 50 menu, click Tools.

2 Click on Contra Entries to bring up the Contra Entries window.

You cannot amend the values shown in the Total boxes.

3 Select Customer (Sales Ledger) and Supplier (Purchase Ledger) accounts.

If your totals do not match, a warning message appears asking whether you want to make part-Contra Entries for the lowest amount. If acceptable click the Yes button or No to cancel the Contra Entries.

4 Select outstanding invoice (on sales side) from the list.

5 Select invoice to apply Contra Entry for.

6 Click OK to finish.

Run Period End Functions

If program date needs changing for Month End procedure, select Change Program Date from the Settings menu. Remember to re-set the date back to the correct date.

Period End options are essential monthly and year end procedures for updating the accounting system, for example, for posting accruals, prepayments and depreciation. The Audit Trail can then be cleared of any unwanted transactions whilst stock can be cleared from your Product history if you so wish.

Through running these procedures, you will also be preparing Sage Line 50 so that you are ready to enter transactions for the new financial year.

Month End

At each month end it is important to post your prepayments, accruals and depreciation values. Sage Line 50 will process these transactions automatically and update your nominal account records and audit trail. The option also exists to clear down your month to date turnover figures for your customer and supplier records.

Always Backup your data files before and after Month End procedures.

Once you have run the Month End procedures, this is an opportune time to produce some of your financial reports, for example, the Profit and Loss, Balance Sheet, Trial Balance, Budget and Prior Year Analysis reports. Customer statements and Aged analysis reports for Debtors and Creditors will also prove useful.

Month End Guidelines

Here is a check list for the Month End:

Use File Maintenance Check and Compress Data options to check your files.

1   Check all relevant transactions have been posted.

2   Check recurring entries have been set up and processed.

3   Check prepayments, accruals and depreciation have been set up.

4   Complete your bank reconciliation.

Refer to Sage Line 50 Library Help system for more information about running Month End procedures.

5   Print product history, valuation and profit reports.

6   Post product journals for your profit and loss and balance sheet.

...cont'd

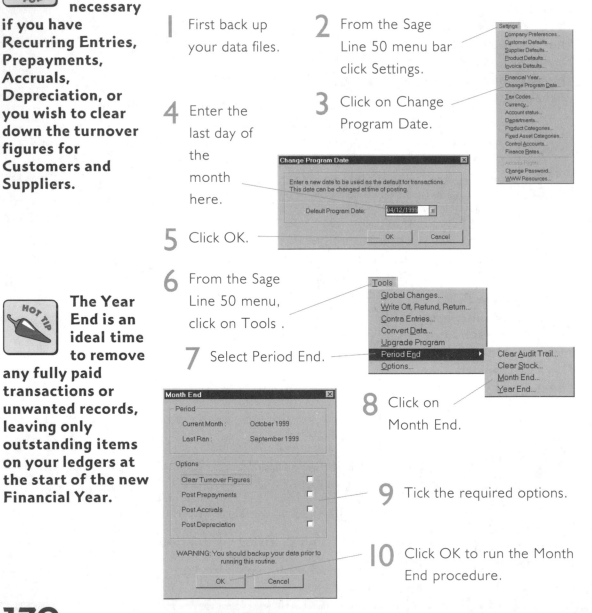

The month end routine is necessary **if you have Recurring Entries, Prepayments, Accruals, Depreciation, or you wish to clear down the turnover figures for Customers and Suppliers.**

After following the Month End guidelines it is time to run the month end procedure. You will probably want to run it on a day other than the actual last calendar day of the month, as this is often more convenient. You will therefore have to change the program date first. To do this, simply follow these steps:

1 First back up your data files.

2 From the Sage Line 50 menu bar click Settings.

3 Click on Change Program Date.

4 Enter the last day of the month here.

5 Click OK.

6 From the Sage Line 50 menu, click on Tools .

7 Select Period End.

8 Click on Month End.

9 Tick the required options.

10 Click OK to run the Month End procedure.

The Year End is an ideal time to remove **any fully paid transactions or unwanted records, leaving only outstanding items on your ledgers at the start of the new Financial Year.**

For additional information about running the Year End Procedure and Checklist refer to the Library Help system.

Take at least two backups of your data files before and after running the Year End routine.

Use File Maintenance to check for errors, correct and compress data files and maximise disk space.

After Year End check your Financial Year Start Date is correct before entering new transactions.

Year End

Before you run the Year End, Month End procedures must first be completed, together with any final adjustments.

First, when you run Month End on the last month of the current financial year, DO NOT clear the Audit Trail. Once values for the month end have been checked and you are satisfied that they are correct, set the program date to the last date of the current financial year and run Year End:

1 Set the program date to the last day of the financial year by doing Steps 1–5 on Page 170.

2 From the Sage Line 50 menu, click on Tools .

3 Select Period End.

4 Click on Year End.

5 Tick here to update your budget figures for each nominal ledger profit and loss account and each product record with the actual values from the year just ending.

6 Change Year End Journals Date if necessary.

7 Select Output.

8 Click OK to run.

Lastly, remove any unwanted Customer, Supplier, Nominal, Bank and Product records and reset date. You are now ready to enter transactions for the new financial year.

Clearing the Audit Trail and Stock

Only paid, allocated and reconciled transactions are removed from the Audit Trail.

The VAT and Bank columns must display the reconciled flag R to be removed from the Audit Trail.

Before running the Clear Stock option, you should back up your data and print your stock valuation and stock history reports. Do likewise before clearing the Audit Trail.

This option lets you remove paid and reconciled transactions prior to a specified date from the Audit Trail. This makes the ledgers easier to read. Reconciled transactions on the nominal ledger are brought forward as opening balances.

Sage Line 50 can store up to 2,000,000,000 transactions in the Audit Trail, so transactions do not have to be removed, but by deleting unwanted transactions, it will free disk space and provide faster access to information.

1 From the Tools menu, select Period End and click Clear Audit Trail.

2 Enter required date.

3 Click OK to clear the Audit Trail.

Clear Stock

This option can be run as part of the Month End and Year End procedures. It allows you to decide when to clear transactions from your Product History.

1 From the Tools menu, select Period End and click Clear Stock.

2 Click Yes to continue.

3 Enter date here.

4 Click OK.

Departmental reporting and activity will be effected by removing transactions from the Audit Trail.

The Task Manager

This chapter shows you how to use the Task Manager for setting up useful functions such as a reminder list of tasks to do, i.e., bills to pay, people to contact, etc. It also lets you quickly view the status of your accounts, invoices, sales orders and purchase orders as well as check how much you owe and vice versa.

Covers

Features of the Tasks Option | 174

The Task Manager Desktop | 175

Setting up a To Do task | 176

Recording a new Bill | 177

Paying a Bill | 178

Accounts Due | 179

Account Status | 180

The Recurring Option | 181

Stock Option | 182

Invoices Option | 183

Sales Order Processing | 184

Purchase Order Processing | 185

The Company Stack | 186

Chapter Fifteen

Features of the Tasks Option

Use the Contacts option to check the people you need to speak to, or have spoken with recently, plus any overdue calls that need making. This information is linked directly to the customer and supplier record Contacts tab and will update the relevant future, today, overdue and completed contacts folder.

Use the Tasks option to set up a list of jobs that you need to do and to prompt you of any tasks that are currently due, overdue or recently completed. By setting up these tasks it acts as a reminder of the actions you need to take to run your business efficiently, produces important information and saves valuable time.

You can use the Tasks option to help you:

- Set up a list of tasks that you need to do and also view any tasks that are either completed, due or overdue.

- List people you need to contact today or in the future, or record and view any contacts that you have 'completed' or that are 'overdue'.

- Record the bills you receive and view bills that are paid, due for payment or overdue.

- Check how much you owe your suppliers and, more important, find out how much you are owed by your customers.

- Check the account status of your customers and suppliers. For example, you will be able to see at a glance which accounts are over the credit limit, inactive or on-hold.

- View and keep track of any recurring entries you have set up in Sage Line 50.

- Quickly check the status of invoices, sales orders and purchase orders. For example, you may want to see which invoices or credit notes are due for printing or which have yet to be posted.

- Keep track of your stock levels. You can easily and quickly check for out of stock items, items which are below re-order level, on order or which have been allocated.

From the Company Stack you can view the company information you entered either in the Startup Wizard or in the Company Preferences option from the Sage Line 50 Settings menu.

The Task Manager Desktop

Your Sage Line 50 Task Manager desktop features a menu bar, a stacked toolbar, an application toolbar and a split screen, with tree view on the left and list view on the right.

From the desktop you can set up tasks, remind yourself of jobs to do etc. To bring up the desktop do the following:

The Application toolbar contains different options with different functions, depending upon the Tasks chosen from the Stacked toolbar.

Options available from the Application toolbar are also available from the Tasks menu. These include New, Open, Delete, Pay and Properties.

Use the List View screen (right hand side of the screen) as a shortcut to your tasks, transactions, bills, recurring entries etc. by simply double-clicking on the required entry.

1 From the Sage Line 50 toolbar, click on the Tasks button.

2 The Menu Bar provides a list of options using drop-down menus.

3 The stacked toolbar area.

4 List View area.

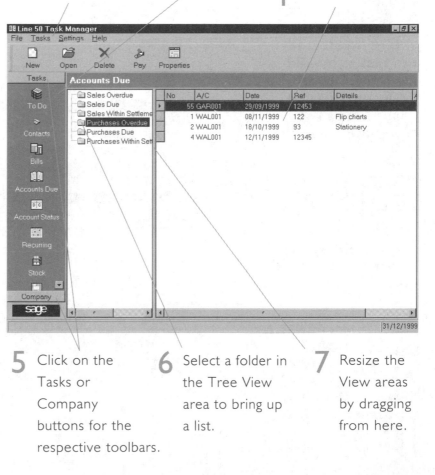

5 Click on the Tasks or Company buttons for the respective toolbars.

6 Select a folder in the Tree View area to bring up a list.

7 Resize the View areas by dragging from here.

Setting up a To Do task

Use the shortcut key CTRL+N, or click the right hand mouse button and select New from the pop-up menu to set up a new To Do task.

Use the To Do option to create a list of tasks you need to complete. The type of tasks include a General Reminder, Send overdue letters, Print management reports etc. Any additional information that may prove useful can be entered within the Description and Notes boxes.

Once saved, the task appears in the Current Tasks folder on the To Do list. This list can then be viewed at any time. To set up a To Do task, proceed as follows:

If the Task Complete box is selected, the task is moved from the Current Tasks or Overdue Tasks list to the Complete Tasks list.

1 From the Task Manager, click on the To Do option from the Tasks stacked toolbar.

2 Click New from the application toolbar.

4 Enter date when task is due for completion.

3 Select the reminder type from the drop down list box.

When you save your task it appears in the Current Tasks folder on the To Do List.

To delete a task, highlight it from the Current, Overdue, or Completed Tasks and click Delete from the File menu.

5 Enter a suitable Description, e.g., chase overdue payments.

6 Type any special instructions here.

7 Click OK to save.

8 Check here when complete.

Recording a new Bill

 When the bill details are saved, it will appear in the Current Bills folder on the Bills list. If required you can edit your bill details.

 Once the Bills option has been selected from the Tasks stacked toolbar, you can use the shortcut key CTRL+N to record a new bill.

 References entered into the Ref box will appear in the Audit Trail for cross referencing purposes.

 If a bill is not paid by the Due Date entered, the task is moved to the Overdue Bills folder.

The Bills option provides a useful and convenient way of recording all your bills, such as rates, rent, etc. Once the payment information is entered and saved, the bill will appear in the Current Bills folder on the Bills list. These details can be edited if required at this stage.

Use the Task Manager then to quickly view which bills are paid, due or overdue. To record a new bill:

1 Using Task Manager, click on the Bills option from the Tasks stacked toolbar.

2 Click New from the File menu.

3 Enter the nominal code for paying the bill to, e.g., if paying your telephone bill the default nominal ledger account is 7502.

4 Describe your transaction here.

Bill Record

Nominal/Category Details

Pay To

Details

Details		Ref
Net	0.00	Tax Code T1 17.50	Vat	0.00
Bill date	31/12/1999	Due date 31/12/1999

Payment Details

Amount 0.00   Date paid / /   Outstanding 0.00

OK   Cancel

5 Enter Net amount of the bill here.

6 Enter date bill received.

7 Enter date bill is due to be paid.

8 Check all Details and click OK to save.

Paying a Bill

After paying a selected bill, it is moved from the Current Bills or Overdue Bills folder to the Paid Bills folder. The bill payment details are updated on the Bill Record.

Use the Pay option to quickly and easily pay any current/ outstanding bills which have been previously set up using Task Manager. To action bill payment the only detail required is the Bank Account nominal code you want to pay the bill from, as follows:

1 Select Bills from the Tasks stacked toolbar.

2 Select either Current Bills or Overdue Bills folder from the Tree view.

3 Select the bill required from the List View.

4 Click the Pay option from the application toolbar.

Bill Payment

Bank Account

Bank `1200` `Bank Current Account`

Payment Details

Ref `INV10002` Date `31/12/1999`

Net `550.26` Tax Code `T1 17.50` Vat `96.30`

OK   Cancel

5 Enter nominal code of Bank account to pay the bill from.

6 Click OK to pay the bill.

An alternative way to pay a bill is by selecting the Pay option from the Application toolbar.

7 The bill is now paid and moves into the Paid Bills folder.

8 Click on the Paid Bills folder and double-click on the bill you have just paid.

Bill Record

Nominal/Category Details

Pay To `7500` `Printing`

Details

Details `Bill Payment` Ref `INV10002`

Net `550.26` Tax Code `T1 17.50` Vat `96.30`

Bill date `30/11/1999` Due date `31/12/1999`

Payment Details

Amount `646.56` Date paid `31/12/1999` Outstanding `0.00`

OK   Cancel

9 Note the Bill Record is updated to show payment details.

10 Click OK to close.

Accounts Due

To view more details about a transaction, select the transaction and use shortcut key ALT+ENTER.

Use the Account Due option from the Tasks stack to identify who owes you money, i.e., Sales Overdue, Sales Due and Sales Within Settlement. You can also check who you owe money to by viewing the Purchases Overdue, Purchases Due and Purchases Within Settlement folders.

To find out which customers owe you money

1 From the Tasks stacked toolbar, select Accounts Due and click the Sales Overdue folder.

Use the Phone button to auto-matically dial your customer telephone number. Your computer (with modem) needs to share the same line as your telephone.

2 Note transaction list of overdue payments.

3 For more details, select a transaction.

4 Click Properties from the application toolbar.

To view details of different transactions on the list, click the First, Previous, Next or Last buttons.

Transaction Details

Account Details

A/C	PEL01	Name	Palmer Energy Ltd
No.	12	Contact	Alan Volt
		Telephone	01987 345345

Values

Net 1079.60
Tax 188.93
Paid 0.00

1268.53

Transaction Details

| Type | Sales Invoice | Ref | 1 |
| Details | | Date | 28/10/1999 |

First   Previous   Next   Last   OK

5 The Transaction Details window appears.

For a printout of debtors refer to the Customers Reports window.

6 Use these buttons to move between different transactions in the list.

7 When finished click OK.

Account Status

The Account Status option lets you view accounts that match certain criteria, for example, Sales Over Credit Limit, Sales On Hold, Purchase Over Credit Limit or Purchase On Hold. If you require more detailed information about a transaction, select it and click the Properties button from the application toolbar.

 Use the shortcut key ALT+ENTER to view transaction properties.

I From the Line 50 Task Manager window, choose the Account Status option from the Tasks stacked toolbar.

 In the Account Details window use the First, Previous, Next and Last buttons to move between different account transactions.

2 Select the folder you require from the Tree View list.

3 Highlight the required account from the List view.

4 Click the Properties button on the application toolbar.

 Use the telephone button to let Sage Line 50 dial a customer for you when you want to speak to them about their account.

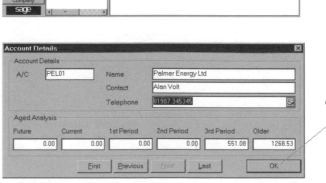

5 When finished, click OK to exit.

The Recurring Option

To set up recurring entries, select the Recurring option from the Bank toolbar.

Using the Task Manager you can view any recurring entries you have set for various transaction types, namely Receipt, Payment, Journal Debit or Journal Credit.

You can view the individual details about the transactions, but you cannot change these details. To view details about a recurring payment you set up in Sage Line 50, do the following:

1 From the Line 50 Task Manager window, choose the Recurring option from the Tasks stacked toolbar.

2 Select the folder you require from the Tree View list, e.g., Payments.

You cannot change your recurring entry details from within the Task Manager.

3 Highlight the required payment from the List view.

4 Click the Properties button on the application toolbar.

5 The details appear for the selected recurring entry.

HOT TIP

For detailed information about recurring entries, select transaction and choose the Properties option from the application toolbar.

Recurring Entry Properties ☒

Details

Trans. Type	Bank Payment	
Bank A/C	1200	Bank Current Account
Nominal Code	2310	Hire Purchase
Ref	DD/STO	Details Hire Purchase Agreement
Department	0 - ** Not Applicable **	
Day to post	28	
Last Posted	28/12/1999	☐ Suspend Posting

Amounts

Net Amount	150.00	Tax Code	T9 0.00	VAT	0.00

Close

---

6 Click Close when finished.

Stock Option

The Task Manager is a handy way of keeping track of your stock. It provides you with a fast and efficient way of seeing what is out of stock, below the reorder level, on order and allocated.

By using Task Manager for regular monitoring of stock you can make decisions about items which need re-ordering or stock you are waiting for.

Stock transactions are for viewing only; a properties facility is not available.

| Select the Stock option from the Tasks stacked toolbar.

Sage Line 50 can only provide accurate reporting and stock tracking if the correct information has been entered in the first place. Plan to make full use of Sage Line 50's extensive stock details recording facilities.

Use the horizontal and vertical scroll bars to view all transaction details.

2 Select the folder required in the Tree View.

3 Relevant details appear in the list area for your information.

4 Click here to scroll across all the details.

Invoices Option

An alternative way to view your invoices is to select Tasks from the Task Manager menu bar and click Invoices.

Within Task Manager you can view the status of any invoices or credit notes that you have recorded.

Invoices and credit notes are listed separately depending on whether they have been printed or posted. You can also quickly view which invoices or credit notes need printing or posting.

For example, do the following to quickly view a list of invoices which you have not yet printed:

1 From the Task Manager window, click on the down button on the Tasks stacked toolbar until Invoices appears.

To print/ post an invoice or credit note or record an invoice/credit note number, return to the Invoicing option on the Sage Line 50 toolbar then select your transaction and use the Print option.

2 Click on the Invoices option.

3 Select Inv to Print folder.

Properties function is not available when viewing invoices or credit notes in the Task Manager.

4 A list of invoices not yet printed appears.

Sales Order Processing

You can also access Sales Orders by selecting Tasks from the Task Manager menu and clicking Sales Orders.

From Task Manager you can view the status of your Sales Orders directly. A selection of folders is available for you to view the type of sales orders required, for example, orders that are 'To Allocate', 'Cancelled', 'Held', etc.

(It is important to remember, however, that you can only view the details in this screen. If you need to create a new Sales Order or make any changes, you will have to return to the SOP option in Sage Line 50).

As an example, if you wanted a list of completed Sales Orders, you could use the SOP Reports facility to print out a suitable report, or you can do a quick view from the Task Manager as follows:

1 From Task Manager, click the SOP option on the Tasks Stacked toolbar.

2 Select the Completed folder.

You will need to return to the SOP option on the Sage Line 50 toolbar to perform any sales order functions.

3 A list of Completed Sales Orders appears in the View area.

Purchase Order Processing

Just as with Sales Orders, use the Task Manager to quickly display the status of your Purchase Orders when you do not need a printed copy. Options available are To Order and To Deliver.

To access Purchase Orders from the Task Manager menu, select Tasks and click Purchase Orders.

For example, to view a list of Purchase Orders that are 'To Deliver' follow these simple steps:

1 From the Task Manager window, choose the POP option from the Tasks stacked toolbar (you may have to use the down button on the stacked toolbar to bring it into view).

2 Select the To Deliver folder in the Tree View.

You cannot alter transaction details using this Task Manager facility. You will need to return to the POP option on the Sage Line 50 toolbar to perform any purchase order functions.

3 A list of Purchase Orders To Deliver appears in the View area.

The Company Stack

This feature is useful for quickly viewing your Company Details, such as Name, Address, Telephone, Fax, VAT Reg. No., Web Site and E-mail.

You can also select Company Details from the Settings menu on the Line 50 Task Manager toolbar to view your Company Details.

These details, however, cannot be edited using this screen. To do so you will need to exit from the Task Manager and return to Sage Line 50. Then, select Company Preferences from the Sage Line 50 Settings menu and make your changes using the Address tab (see page 11).

To quickly view Company Details from the Task Manager just do the following:

1 Click on the Company button at the foot of the stacked toolbar.

2 Click on Company Details to view information.

3 The Details window appears.   4 Click OK to close.

Index

A

Account Status   13
Accounts Due   179
Accounts Status   180
Accruals   53
Activity   23
  Supplier   37
Adjustments In   84
Adjustments Out   84
Aged Balances   38
  Customer   23
  Supplier   38
Allocating Stock   105
Assemblies   80
Assets. *See also* Fixed Assets
  Depreciation   137
  Valuation   138
Audit Trail   121–122
  Clearing the Audit Trail   172

B

Backing up   156
Balance Sheet   125
Bank   57–72
  Account Types   59
    Bank, Cash, and Credit   60
  Batch Purchase Payments   63
  Cheques   68
  Customer Receipts   65
  Payments   61
  Receipts   64
  Reconciliation   70–71
    Making Adjustments   71
  Recurring Entries   67
  Reports   72
  Statement   69
  Supplier Invoice Payments   62

  Toolbar   58
  Transfers   66
Bank Account
  Opening Balances   152
Bank Account Reconciliation   70
Bank Statement   69
Bank Transfers   66
Batch
  Customer Credit Notes   25
  Customer Invoices   24
  Supplier Credit Notes   40
  Supplier Invoices   39
Bill of Materials   80
Budget Report   127

C

Calculations   139
Cash Account   60
Categories
  Departments   11
  Fixed Asset   11
  Fixed Assets   135
  Product   11, 75
Changing Program Date   170
Chart of Accounts   54–55
Cheque Returns   167
Cheques   68
Clearing Opening Balances   149
Clearing Stock   172
Comma Separated Values   160
Company Preferences   11
Company Stack   186
Contacts   22, 35
Contacts Option   174
Contra Entries   168
Control Accounts   16
Correcting Transactions   163
Corruption of Data   156

Credit Card account   60
Credit Charges   27
Credit Control   22
Credit Note   40
  Product   96
  Service   97
Credit Note Status   183
Criteria   36, 49, 79, 139
CSV (Comma Separated Values) files   160
Currency   14
Current Liquidity   126
Customer Defaults   15
Customer Ledger   19–32
  Activity   23
  Batch credit notes   25
  Batch Invoices   24
  Debtors Analysis   26
  Disputed Invoices   28
  Labels   31
  Letters   30
  Phone   29
  Records   22–23
  Reports   29
  Statement   32
  Toolbar   21

D

Data Compression   164
Data Management   155–172
  Backing up   156
  Clearing Stock   172
  Clearing the Audit Trail   172
  Contra Entries   168
  File Maintenance   162–164
  Global Values   158–159
  Importing Data   160–161
  Period End Functions   169–171
  Restoring Data   157
  Write Off, Refund and Return   165–167
Debit   50
Debtors Analysis   26
Defaults

Customer   15
Product   16
Supplier   15
Departments   11
Depreciation   137
  Reducing Balance   135
  Straight Line   135
  Write Off   135
Despatching Sales Orders   106
Disputed Invoices   28
Double-Entry Bookkeeping   50

E

Easy Startup Wizard   11
Error Checking   162
Error Corrections   163
Euro   14
Euro Calculator   14

F

File Maintenance   162
Filters   139
Finance Rates   17
Financial Systems   20
Financial Year   13
Financials   119–132
  Audit Trail   121–122
  Balance Sheet   125
  Budget Report   127
  Printing the Audit Trail   122
  Prior Year Report   128
  Profit and Loss Report   124
  Quick Ratio   126
  Recording your Fixed Assets   135
  Reports   132
  Toolbar   120
  Trial Balance   123
  VAT Return   129–131
  VAT Transfer Wizard   131
Fixed Asset Categories   11

Fixed Assets 133–138
  Depreciation 137
  Fixed Asset Records 136
  Toolbar 134
  Valuation 138

G

Getting Started 7–18
  Company Preferences 11
  Currency & the Euro 14
  Customer & Supplier Defaults 15
  Finance Rates 17
  Introduction 8
  Sage Line 50 Toolbar 18
  Settings 10
  Starting Sage Line 50 9
Global Values 158
Graphs 47
Grouping 142

H

HM Customs & Excise 129

I

Importing Data 160
Introduction 8
Invoice Status 183
Invoices 87–100
  Invoicing 89
  Printing an invoice 92
  Printing batch invoices 99
  Product 90–91
  Product Credit Note 96
  Reports 100
  Service 93–94
  Service Credit Note 97
  Skeleton 95
  Toolbar 88
  Updating 98

J

Journal 50
  Credit 50
  Debit 50
  Journal Entry 51
  Skeleton Journals 50

L

Labels 31, 41
Layout and Format 139
Letters 30, 41

M

Making Adjustments 71
Modifying an existing Report 144
Month End 169–170
  Guidelines 169
  Procedure 170
Multiple Document Windows 140

N

New
  Bank Wizard 59
  Customer Wizard 22
  Nominal Account Wizard 45
  Product Wizard 76
  Report 141
  Supplier Wizard 35
Nominal Ledger 43–56
  Accruals 53
  Activity 48
  Chart of Accounts 54–55
  Graphs 47
  Making a Journal Entry 51
  Nominal accounts 45
  Opening Balances 152
  Prepayments 52

Records 46
Reports 56
The Journal 50
Toolbar 44
Transaction Codes/Types 49
Viewing Nominal Transactions 47–49

O

On Order 113
Opening Balances 145–154
  Brought Forward 172
  Clearing O/B from Trial Balance 149–150
  Entering O/B during the Year 151
  Introduction 146
  Nominal Ledger and Bank Account 152–153
  Products 154
  Standard VAT 147
  VAT Cash Accounting 148

P

Page Footer 142
Page Header 142
Passwords 10
Payments 57
  Batch Purchase 63
  Supplier Invoice 62
  To Bank 61
Period End Functions 169
Phone 29
Placing Orders Manually 115
Pre-printed Stationery 140
Prepayments 52
Previewing your Report 143
Printing
  Batched Purchase Orders 117
  Invoices 92
    Batch invoices 99
  Sales Orders 107

Prior Year Report 128
Products 73–86
  Activity 82
  Adjustments 84
  Bill of Materials 80
  Categories 75
  Credit Note 96
  Defaults 16, 78
  Discounts 81
  Invoicing 90–91
  Opening Balances 154
  Record 75–77
  Reports 86
  Toolbar 74
  Transfers 85
  Using Criteria 79
  Viewing Transactions 81
Profit and Loss Report 124
Purchase Order Deliveries
  Recording Deliveries 114
Purchase Order Processing 109–118
  Manual Deliveries 116
  On Order 113
  Place Manually On Order 115
  Printing 117
  Purchase Order 111–112
  Reports 118
  Toolbar 110

Q

Quick Ratio 126

R

Rebuild 164
Receipts
  Bank 64
  Customer 65
Recording Deliveries Manually 116
Recording Stock Deliveries
  Automatically 114
Records

Bank   59
Customer   22
Nominal   46
Product   75
Supplier   35
Recurring Entries   67
Recurring Option   181
Refunds   165
Report Designer   139–144
Calculations   139
Creating a new Report   141
Criteria   139
Filters   139
Grouping   142
Introduction   140
Layout and Format   139
Modifying an existing Report   144
Printing   140
Report Wizard   141
Sort Variables   141
Stationery   140
Totals   141
Report Variables   141
Reports
Bank   72
Customer   29
Financial   132
Fixed Assets   135
Invoicing   100
Nominal   56
Products   86
Purchase Orders   118
Sales Orders   108
Suppliers   42
Restoring Data   157
Returns   165
Reversing VAT Reconciled
Transactions   164

S

Sage Line 50 Desktop   9
Sage Line 50 Toolbar   7
Sales Order Processing   101–108
Allocating Stock   105
Amending   107
Despatching   106
Printing   107
Reports   108
Sales Order   103–104
Toolbar   102
Sales Order Status   184
Service Credit Note   97
Service Invoice   93–94
Settings   10
Account Status   13
Company Preferences   11
Control Accounts   16
Currency   14
Customer Defaults   15
Departments   11
Finance Rates   17
Financial Year   13
Fixed Asset   11
Passwords   10
Product   11
Product Defaults   16
Supplier Defaults   15
Tax Codes   12
Shortcut Keys   10
Skeleton Invoice   95
Skeleton Journals   50
Stacked Toolbar   175
Standard VAT Opening Balances   147
Start up check List   8
Statement   32
Stationery   140
Stock
Allocation   105
Clearing Stock   172
Stock Status Option   182
Supplier Defaults   15

Supplier Ledger   33–42
  Activity   37
  Aged Balance   38
  Batch Invoices   39
  Credit Notes   40
  Labels   41
  Letters   41
  Records   35
  Reports   42
  Toolbar   34
  Using Criteria   36

T

Task Manager   173–186
  Accounts Due   179
  Accounts Status   180
  Application Toolbar   175
  Company Stack   186
  Desktop   175
  Features of Tasks Options   174
  Invoices Option   183
  List View   175
  Paying a Bill   178
  Purchase Order Status   185
  Recording a new Bill   177
  Recurring Option   181
  Sales Order Status   184
  Setting up a To Do task   176
  Stacked Toolbar   175
  Stock Option   182
  Tree View   175
Task Manager Desktop   175
Tax Codes   12
Telephoning your Customers   29
Transaction Types   23, 37, 49, 82
  Customer   23
  Nominal   49
  Product   82
  Supplier   37
Tree View   175
Trial Balance   123
  Clearing Opening Balances   149

U

Updating your Ledgers   98

V

Valuation of Fixed Assets   138
VAT Cash Accounting Opening
  Balances   148
VAT Numbers   11, 22, 35, 186
VAT Return   129–131
VAT Transfer Wizard   131
Viewing Transactions   37, 47, 81

W

Windows Desktop   9
Wizards
  Bank Account   59
  Customer   22
  Easy Startup Wizard   11
  Nominal Account   45
  Product   76
  Supplier   35
  VAT Transfer Wizard   131
Write Off, Refund and Return   165
Write Offs   167
WWW Details   11, 22, 35, 186

Y

Year End Procedure   171